Camino de Santiago

TO WALK FAR, CARRY LESS

Jean-Christie Ashmore

CAMINO DE SANTIAGO

TO WALK FAR, CARRY LESS

JEAN-CHRISTIE ASHMORE

With thanks to those who help us find The Way

Trail markers made by volunteers from Camino associations, local municipalities, and French and Spanish citizens who live near the pilgrimage trails. The scallop shell is the ancient Camino symbol.

TABLE OF CONTENTS

Carrying Less: How to Create a Lightweight Camino Backpack

What to Wear on a Camino Pilgrimage

What to Carry in a Camino Backpack

INTRODUCTION

"We carry our fears in our backpacks." That's what Vidal, a Spanish pilgrim, told me over a decade ago.

I first noticed him in Roncesvalles, a medieval village set in the Pyrenees Mountains near the border between France and Spain. It was the starting point for my first Camino pilgrimage, and Vidal captured my attention because he looked like a medieval pilgrim: A floppy felt hat sat low on his head, and a large hand gripped a walking staff that rose nearly to his shoulders. A scallop shell dangled from a leather thong hung around his neck. That, I thought, is a serious pilgrim.

I wasn't a pilgrim—yet. And I knew little about the Camino de Santiago (I wasn't yet using the internet). I figured I was going on a recreational backpacking adventure, and I thought the experience would be similar to my previous backpacking journeys. So I packed my old sturdy backpack using my already fine-tuned pack list for what I imagined would be a lightweight backpack. Then I added more—the "I might need this," or "what if that happens," or "what if I can't find this on the Camino" type of things. And after that I added some "this might be nice to have" items.

By day two on the Camino, I was a wreck. I had become so discouraged from blisters and inflamed calves that I was already debating whether I should just quit the Camino. That afternoon Vidal appeared on the trail as I was bandaging blisters, and he noticed my woe-is-me face—and my huge backpack. He sat down to chat for a while, and then with great sympathy he offered his tactful and indirect advice about carrying one's fears in a backpack.

He was right: I had so much of that might-need, what-if, and nice-to-have stuff (aka fears) in my pack that my sleeping bag had to be strapped to the outside bottom of my backpack. With every step it slapped me in the derriere.

That night I threw out everything but the essentials needed for the Camino journey, and the spanking ended. I felt lighter on my feet, and my enthusiasm for the Camino returned. Five weeks later I walked into the city of Santiago de Compostela with a fitness I hadn't felt for years—and a soaring spirit inspired by the beauty of the landscapes I'd traveled through and the fun camaraderie I had experienced with other pilgrims. My pack was lighter, and so was I. It's not an unusual feeling after completing the Camino journey: Vidal told me he'd felt like a backpack had been thrown from his soul after his first Camino pilgrimage.

I had become a pilgrim after all, and the journey had become more than just a recreational backpacking adventure. That first Camino experience was the beginning of my passion for walking the old Camino pilgrimage routes in France and Spain. On subsequent journeys I picked up tips and advice from experienced backpackers and found myself carrying an increasingly lighter load, often to the point where I noticed my pack no more than I noticed the hat upon my head.

Learning to pack light has helped me to walk, so far, about 2,400 kilometers (over 1,500 miles) on the Camino. But that's not a boast. My numbers are low compared to others I've met, and besides, the point of the Camino is not to rack up kilometers to suit the ego. The Camino has the potential to change lives and to restore both body and soul.

Most of the tens of thousands of men and women who walk the Camino each year have never before gone on a long-distance backpacking journey. And while Camino guidebooks provide helpful details for the routes, they rarely provide information to fully answer this question: "What should I take on a Camino pilgrimage?" Nor do they offer advice or tips on how to prepare a lightweight backpack.

Everyone starts their Camino pilgrimage hoping they'll walk for days, weeks, or months. But I've seen too many pilgrims—whether they're twenty years old or sixty—stop their journey short because of physical problems like inflamed knees, Achilles tendonitis, or severe blisters, to name a few of the most common maladies. Although an overloaded backpack may not directly cause these problems, carrying too much weight can certainly exacerbate them to the point where it's impossible to continue.

A heavy backpack can also diminish a pilgrim's enthusiasm. Imagine walking up and down steep hills, or even on flat terrain, for several hours—hiking the Camino typically requires walking for at least five hours per day—while carrying a heavy pack. The Camino is arduous enough without carrying what constantly feels like a burden on your back.

THE BENEFITS OF A LIGHTER LOAD

- You can use a backpack without the features needed to support heavy loads, such as internal frames, that make the pack itself heavier. This alone could save you half a kilogram (a pound)—or more.
- You won't need to wear heavy boots to support the weight of a heavy pack.
- You're less likely to experience strain on your feet, ankles, knees, back, shoulders, and hips.
- You'll have better balance and agility when crossing creeks and walking in slippery mud or on rocky paths.
- You're more likely to stay enthusiastic about the Camino while walking long distances, day after day, in all kinds of weather and on all types of terrain.

In this book you'll find answers to the question of what to take on a Camino pilgrimage. Everything—from what to wear (including footwear and socks) to what to carry in your backpack—is covered. You'll see detailed descriptions, options to consider, and the pros and cons for some of the choices you need to make (e.g., poncho or rain jacket? sleeping bag or sleeping sheet? water bottles or built-in hydration system? and what about mobile phones and other tech gear?). And even if you don't want to pack a super-lightweight backpack, this book offers practical packing advice—like how to distribute the weight in your backpack—that can help you prepare your Camino backpack.

The Camino is for everyone, whether you're rich, poor, or somewhere in between. That's been the Camino tradition for over a thousand years. So for those on a strict budget, there's a separate chapter with ideas on how to save money on, or avoid buying, often-costly outdoor gear.

An example pack list at the end of the book includes the weight of each item. And, unlike many Camino pack lists, you'll see that everything worn and carried is listed—including estimates for picnic lunches, snack foods, and water. These are often the heaviest items carried, so they should be included when calculating the total weight of your backpack. Experienced backpackers call a list of this type the "from the skin out" weight, since it includes everything—even an example of what could be carried in shirt or pants pockets—and how much each item weighs.

This book begins by providing tips and advice on how to pack a lightweight backpack. Then you'll know how to make the best choices for what to take, and what questions you should ask yourself before starting the process of organizing your Camino gear. You'll also learn how to weigh everything, and the best scale to use.

The information in this book will help you better prepare for your Camino pilgrimage, so you arrive safely at your destination feeling fit and as though you've "thrown a backpack from your soul," as Vidal said. He was the first of countless pilgrims who have demonstrated to me over the years the Camino tradition to help and support other pilgrims. It's in that spirit that I hope this book helps you walk far by carrying less.

Buen Camino,
Jean-Christie

A PILGRIM FRIEND TESTS THE EXAMPLE CAMINO PACK LIST
ON THE VÍA DE LA PLATA ROUTE IN SPAIN.

Camino de Santiago (Spanish)
Chemin de Saint-Jacques-de-Compostelle (French)
The Way of Saint James (English)

Over the past one thousand years, millions of people have walked to the Spanish city of Santiago de Compostela following routes affectionately known as The Camino (often called *The Way* in English). And the endless river of people continues: each year tens of thousands of men and women—from students to seniors—take a break from their ordinary lives to walk for days or weeks on the ancient pilgrimage routes throughout western Europe. The most popular of these routes run through France and Spain.

The original inspiration for the Camino pilgrimage tradition started with a legend. Around the year 813 AD, the remains of Apostle James the Greater (later known as Saint James) were said to be buried at the site where the cathedral in Santiago de Compostela,

Spain, stands today. Since then, this legend has inspired members of the Roman Catholic Church to go on a pilgrimage to "Santiago"—Sant Iago is the name for Saint James in the Galician language spoken in northwest Spain. The first Camino guidebook was written in about 1140-1150 AD, and by the twelfth and thirteenth centuries about a half million pilgrims were making their way to Santiago each year, traveling on or near the same routes pilgrims use today.

You'll meet people of all faiths, or of no faith at all, on their way to Santiago. Everyone walks for their own reasons, spiritual or otherwise—and everyone's called a pilgrim on the Camino, whether they're religious or not.

"Give yourself to the Camino," an elderly Spanish man told me over dinner one night on the Camino Francés route. He meant that you might find that the Camino turns into more than just a cheap and fun vacation. Walking for days or weeks gives you the time to sort life out—whether it's to soothe a grief, exhaust a grudge, make an important decision, seek new insights, or to simply recharge your precious life spirit. You can rest your soul on the Camino. Yet the "fun" part is unavoidable: many will say that making new friends with pilgrims from all over the world was the best part of their journey. Most pilgrims also return home with a physical fitness perhaps not felt in years.

Many, including women of all ages, will set out alone on the Camino, knowing they'll easily meet others on the way—especially at the most popular starting points. Others go with a partner, spouse, friend, group of friends, parent, or child. You can always find someone not too far behind or ahead of you on the most-traveled French and Spanish routes.

Pilgrims rely on guidebooks for detailed trail directions and for options on where to eat and sleep (you don't need to carry camping gear on the Camino). Guidebooks also tell you where you can find help, transportation, water, and shops, and will point out important historical sites.

IT'S NOT VERY OFTEN THAT YOU'LL SEE A SOLO PILGRIM ON THE
MOST POPULAR ROUTE IN SPAIN, THE CAMINO FRANCÉS.

It can take about five to seven weeks to walk an entire route through France to the Spanish border. It takes about the same amount of time to walk across Spain to Santiago de Compostela. Pilgrims with limited vacation time, however, will walk only part of a route. It's your journey, and you can choose to start and finish it wherever you like.

Regardless of their faith or how long they've been walking, most pilgrims experience an extraordinary joy when they finally see the tall spires of the magnificent cathedral rising over the city of Santiago de Compostela. Weary feet are suddenly energized to walk only a few kilometers more to arrive at this historic pilgrimage destination. Surely that's something all pilgrims have shared over the past one thousand years—and hopefully will continue to share over the next millennium.

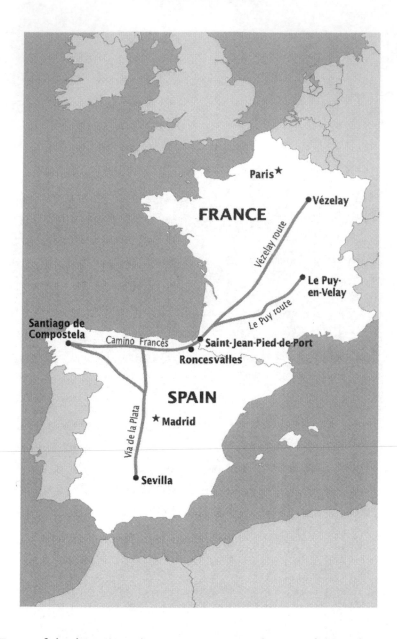

Four of the historic pilgrimage routes where today's pilgrim can find well-marked trails and places to stay—and where solo pilgrims are more likely to meet others.

CARRYING LESS:

How to Create a Lightweight Camino Backpack

CHAPTER 1

AIM FOR 10 PERCENT
Making Choices and Asking Questions

The purpose of this book is not to dictate what exactly should be worn or carried, but rather to present options and to offer suggestions in every possible category. I have my biases and preferences, as do all experienced pilgrims, and you'll have your own preferences as well. But when we follow the lightweight packing methods used by all types of experienced backpackers, not just pilgrims, we can create our own lightweight backpacks—regardless of the specific differences in what we take on a Camino pilgrimage.

These methods are best explained by looking at how to choose Camino gear in the first place, and by asking questions while assembling that gear. And there are a few other tips as well. Let's begin with the best advice—and the toughest to follow—first:

As a general guideline, aim for your backpack's total weight to be 10 percent of your body weight.

Then know it's likely to turn out to be a bit more. This is because Camino pilgrims must also always carry water, and usually a picnic lunch and snack foods, all of which are particularly heavy. For example, one liter of water (about a quart) weighs 1 kilogram (about 2.2 pounds). Of course, the amount of water and food you carry depends on the route, the weather, and your needs.

On the Camino
Sometimes you'll get lucky and get to eat lunch at a rural country inn, where you might try the day's special, such as *rabo del toro* (bull's tail). It's delicious!

While you can't really plan ahead of time for the food and water that you'll need every day, you can estimate what you'll likely carry on average (for more details see Chapter 7: Food and Water).

If you keep the filled pack weight to 10 percent of your body weight—not including food and water—you'll likely end up carrying about 11 or 12 percent of your body weight after adding food and water. Again, that depends on how much food and water you need or want.

The good news: that weight decreases as you consume the water and food. By the afternoon, when you're most fatigued, your pack will weigh less.

Packing Tips

Assemble all of your gear before getting a backpack. That way you can choose the best backpack size to hold the bulk of your gear. If you're eager to buy something significant that strengthens your commitment to go on a Camino pilgrimage, it's better to buy your footwear before anything else—and then start walking so you can break it in!

After using the 10 percent principle to determine the total weight of your backpack, keep the following points in mind when selecting what to wear and carry on the Camino.

Make Choices That Help You Create a Lightweight Backpack
Choose the Lightest

Mesh bag for clothes instead of a stuff sack. Crocs rather than Tevas. Pants, shirts, and jackets made with lighter fabrics and less features than the sporty alternatives. Vanity sometimes weighs too much. Choose the lightest option that provides the necessary benefits or function.

Choose the Smallest

Choose a travel-size toothbrush, deodorant, and dental floss instead of the regular sizes used at home. You can always buy more along the Camino. Use a small comb or brush, and consider the smaller pack towel. Write in a pocket memo book instead of a large journal. Always choose the smallest size available of the thing you need.

Choose the Simplest

A pullover fleece with no pockets or zipper. A backpack without hooks, compression straps, or daisy chains. Choose the most basic option that meets your needs.

Lightweight Notes

simple designs = fewer materials = less weight

More Tips for Packing a Lightweight Camino Backpack
Eliminate

Rip out guidebook pages you don't need. Knowing about flora and fauna is interesting, not essential. Historical information weighs a lot. Carry route descriptions only.

Write notes in your route guides to consolidate and eliminate pages. Trim the margins to save weight and diminish volume.

Toss out or mail home guidebook pages after using them on the Camino.

Follow the same guidelines for maps. Write notes from the guidebook on your maps to eliminate even more pages.

Type addresses and phone numbers on one sheet of paper instead of carrying an address book.

Cut off all unneeded straps, daisy chains, and ice-pick loops on your backpack. Cut labels off clothing. Cut the plastic heads off stuff-sack drawcords, and tie the cord end into a knot.

Scrutinize every item for ways to cut, trim, tear, or pare.

Put everything you eliminate into a pile to weigh later; you'll be pleased to see how much weight you've saved. On my last Camino journey, I saved 494 grams (1 pound, 1 ounce) just by tearing out guidebook pages and cutting maps.

Find Multiple Uses

Look for a multiple personality in every item when assembling your gear. Socks serve as mittens. Shampoo works as laundry soap. A mobile phone with a camera satisfies simple photography needs.

A bandana is the ultimate multipurpose item: a placemat for a picnic, a pillow cover in a refuge, and bandit-style protection to keep your face warm in cold weather. Wet the bandana and it cools your face when it's hot.

A pack towel becomes a neck scarf in unexpected cold weather. Two socks pinned together with safety pins provide ear cover. Fashion on the Camino? Forget about it. Vanity evaporates in freezing-cold air.

An iPod or mobile phone stores addresses, calendars, even documents, and the light emitted from the screen is a good-enough flashlight to find a toilet in the middle of the night—or you might be able to get a flashlight application installed on your mobile phone.

A mobile phone loaded with a translation app eliminates the need to carry a French or Spanish dictionary or phrase book. Apps for Camino guidebooks are also increasingly available.

Replenish

Everything can be bought in France and Spain. You could set out from home with *nothing,* arrive in France or Spain, and get everything you'd need for a pilgrimage on the Camino. Avoid stocking up on toiletries or other items. You'll find plenty of opportunities to replenish supplies along the Camino. If you can't find a small package of something, see if you can share the larger quantity with another pilgrim. Of course there are exceptions—you may not want to share a tube of toothpaste with someone you don't know well, for example. But by the time you need to replenish something, it's likely your backpack's weight will have diminished because you've used other consumables (like liquid soap or sunscreen lotion), so a larger tube of toothpaste will probably not dramatically change the weight of your backpack.

Caveat: Footwear should be bought well in advance and broken in—or you could experience serious regrets.

Be Firm. Ask Yourself...

- Will I use this every day? Think twice about taking anything that you don't expect to use every single day on the Camino. Exceptions: rain gear, first aid kit, cold-weather clothing, and most likely, a sleeping bag (see the pros and cons of sleeping sheets and sleeping bags in Chapter 6: Sleeping Bag or Sheet?).

- Will I need this? If in doubt, leave it out. Extra clothes for dinner at an expensive restaurant? Not needed: pilgrims of both genders wear their cleanest hiking clothes and hide their boots under white tablecloths while they eat gourmet meals and drink fine wines. On the Camino routes, it's almost always acceptable.

- Will I need this much, or that many? "Don't pack for the worst scenario. Pack for the best scenario and simply buy yourself out of any jams," writes Rick Steves, author of a series of popular guidebooks to Europe. Great advice for any type of traveling.

- Is this a fear? Remember Vidal's words. Are you packing items that represent your fears? I took a small flashlight and a space blanket on *three* different pilgrimages before admitting the truth: I never once used them. I suppose that somewhere in the back of my mind I was afraid of getting lost in the dark woods on a cold night. But of course I learned that the Camino is not the same as a wilderness hike, and that spending a cold night in the woods would probably never happen. The flashlight and the space blanket are gone forever from my Camino pack list.

Now let's look at how to weigh your Camino gear. In order to create a backpack that weighs about 10 percent of your body weight, every single item that you want to carry in your backpack must be weighed, from lip balm to sleeping bag. Sure, it's a hassle to weigh every item, just as it's tough to recognize the difference between the items you *want* and those you truly *need*. But the payoff is worth it.

CHAPTER 2

WEIGHING YOUR CAMINO GEAR
Scales to Use and Tips for Accuracy

Experienced backpackers know that grams quickly add up to kilograms. Weighing each item reveals weight hogs, helping you determine what to bring and what to leave behind.

Once you've weighed everything, you'll be able to choose items wisely based on their weight, instead of debating which shirt or soap to bring based on less important criteria (blue or green shirt? liquid or powder soap?).

For dramatic proof, keep a pile of everything you decide not to take. Weigh that pile after you've finished packing, and you'll see why experienced lightweight backpackers weigh *everything*, from dental floss to footwear.

What to Weigh First

Once you've determined your backpack's weight budget, gather *all* the probable contents of your backpack. Then weigh the essential items first, including the backpack itself. Essential items are the things you'll use every day, as well as some other must-haves such as rain gear and a first aid kit.

A weight budget of 10 percent of your body weight usually doesn't allow for those might-need or nice-to-have items. For now, recognize them as such, and put them in a separate dream pile.

Once you're satisfied with your final pack weight, take another look at that dream pile. Even lightweight backpackers often carry treats or small comforts. Just be sure your nonessentials offer enough satisfaction to justify carrying them for hundreds of kilometers.

I sometimes carry micro-ground instant coffee in my pack because I think it's nice to have. Twelve cups' worth weighs about 46 grams (1.6 ounces)—the small amount of extra weight is worth it for the pleasure it gives to me and to others who'll enjoy a hot cup of coffee on the trail.

Choosing a Scale

A small postal scale, with a weight limit up to 2200 grams (5 pounds), works perfectly for weighing backpacking gear (and so does an accurate kitchen scale, if it has a large enough base to place the items on). A sleeping bag will likely weigh the most, and it shouldn't weigh more than about half of that small postal scale's weight limit.

Postal scales can be found pretty much anywhere office supplies are sold, and they aren't very expensive. I bought my 2200-gram (5-pound) digital postal scale for about $25 (€18). I've used it for weighing food too. (Yes, it gets cleaned between weighing the boots and the pasta!)

Lightweight Notes

Forget the body scale you may have at home. While it could be used to weigh a fully loaded backpack, it won't be able to accurately weigh small items—a tiny bar of soap, a pair of socks, a digital camera, a pocketknife, a bandana—whose individual weight should be considered.

Weighing Tips

It can be awkward to weigh some items on the small weighing platform of the scale. Use a rubber band or string to scrunch up clothing and other items so they fit on the platform. Also weigh the string or rubber band by itself, and deduct its weight from the weight of the item you wrapped it around. Even that minuscule amount makes a difference in the overall totals (perhaps enough to make you feel OK about packing that micro-ground coffee, for example).

Use a computer spreadsheet application to keep a running total as you enter each item's weight. Or make a list on paper with two columns: item and weight. It's best to use a pencil with an eraser, as you'll likely make adjustments.

Digital postal scales usually offer a choice to weigh in grams or ounces. Choose grams: it's easier to add whole numbers than fractions. You'll notice how complicated adding ounces can be in Chapter 16: Example Camino Pack List, where weights are listed in both grams and ounces.

If metric weights seem meaningless to you, convert to ounces after weighing in grams. You can easily find conversions online if you Google, for example, "how many ounces is 500 grams."

Average Versus Actual Weights

When buying items online, look for the weight of an item listed under "Specs" or "Specifications," but be aware that the weights are usually an average. Size differences, for example, will affect the actual weight—pants for a petite woman will weigh less than those for a tall man. If the weight is not indicated online, get it by calling or emailing the retailer. Once you receive the item, weigh it yourself so you'll have a more accurate final tally.

Weighing Your Packed Backpack

The key question: according to the list you made of each item's weight, does your backpack weigh about 10 percent of your body weight *before* food and water?

If not, this is the time to eliminate excess weight. The rest of this book will help in that process by offering specific ideas to reduce weight on each item.

After reaching your weight-budget goal in theory, it's time for the real-world test. To weigh your fully loaded backpack, you'll need a larger-capacity scale than your small postal scale. For the most accurate weight, go to a bank, a fitness center, or a post office. You can also use your body scale at home if you're sure of its accuracy. Product reviews often indicate that these scales are not accurate, however, and inaccuracy will defeat the purpose of having weighed each item individually. Getting an accurate total weight for your pack ensures that your tedious efforts to weigh and write down each item's weight weren't in vain.

Another option is to use a hand-held digital luggage scale. But again, read reviews regarding their accuracy.

Add water and food to your pack—estimate what you'd consume on an average day, including snacks, a picnic lunch, and *at least* one liter of water—for a final, realistic grand total.

———————

Now that you know about the basic methods to create a lightweight backpack, let's look at options, advice, and weight considerations for everything you'll wear and carry on a Camino pilgrimage.

What to
Wear on a Camino
Pilgrimage

CHAPTER 3

CAMINO CLOTHING
How to Stay Warm When It's Cold and Cool When It's Hot

The Camino frees one from fashion concerns. A pilgrim typically has one core outfit that he or she wears every day—for weeks. It's liberating because it's simple. (So is the laundry.)

The challenge is to choose the right clothing so that you'll feel comfortable in a variety of situations. For example, you'll often experience different levels of exertion throughout each day's hike—especially in the hilly or mountainous areas. And, of course, the weather is a big factor. If you're walking for days or weeks, you should be prepared for everything: cold or hot temperatures, rain, and maybe even a surprise dusting of snow. But you'll also want to feel comfortable at night—when going out to dinner, visiting the local sites, and just hanging out inside the pilgrims' refuges, which can range from chilly monasteries to stuffy-when-crowded facilities.

A PILGRIM ENJOYING THE VIEW AT A MEDIEVAL—AND CHILLY-AT-NIGHT—PILGRIMS' REFUGE ALONG THE VÉZELAY ROUTE

First we'll look at a few basic features to consider when choosing Camino clothing. Then I'll explain in depth a system to layer your clothing, since that's the key to staying warm when it's cold, and cool when it's hot, in any Camino situation.

Backpacking Clothes: Three Features to Look For
- **Lightweight:** Several layers of lighter clothing provide more options for staying warm or cooling off than one or two heavy layers. The following section provides more specifics on choosing your layers.
- **Wicking:** Fabrics that pull the sweat from the surface of your skin to evaporate or to be transferred to the next layer of clothing help keep your body dry. You'll feel warmer when it's cold and less sweaty when it's hot.
- **Breathability:** Choose garments that allow body heat to escape. This can be accomplished through design and/or fabric. Breathable fabrics usually have labels indicating as much. As for design, look for features such as a mesh panel located under the arms or on the back of a shirt. Another option: get a larger size than you normally would. That roominess itself provides ventilation.

Four Clothing Layers for a Camino Pilgrimage

There's some debate in the backpacking community about how many layers of clothing backpackers should use. Some say three layers—a base layer, a mid-layer, and a shell—is sufficient for any type of backpacking, but I recommend taking four layers of clothing (plus undergarments) on the Camino—an inner layer, a mid-layer, an insulation layer, and a shell. The difference with my system is this: what I consider to be the mid-layer are your walking clothes for a pleasant-weather day on the Camino, not an insulation layer, and the base layer is for sleeping and for providing extra warmth during very cold weather. I suggest this approach because it provides more layering options for the not-in-the-wilderness Camino journey, while still making it possible to accomplish the lightweight backpack goal. Although it's possible to get by with less on the Camino in summer, you should at least take rain gear as an outer shell layer: summer rains are not uncommon. (Rain gear is such an important topic for Camino pilgrims that it has its own chapter.)

It's also not uncommon to experience cold weather in the summer—day or night, in the mountains or not. Summer storms can make the temperatures drop. That's why I recommend taking warm clothing regardless of when you walk the Camino. Layers provide the most flexibility for both hot and cold temperatures.

Two or three lightweight garments that can be layered are more adaptable than one heavy fleece jacket. Even on a cold day, a Camino pilgrim can get hot, especially when marching up a steep hill. Layers provide the option to peel off just the right amount of clothing to avoid overheating. And you can always layer up again, adding the right amount of clothing to keep your body at a comfortable temperature.

When starting out in the morning, here's a simple way to test your layers: if you're warm and cozy while standing still, you'll likely overheat once you start walking. Take a layer off. If you continue to warm up while walking, remove additional layers. When you stop for a break or a picnic lunch, add layers again to prevent getting chilled while in repose.

Not Considered a Layer: Undergarments
Underpants

Why it's called a "pair" when it's just one thing, I don't know. But I take three pairs: one to wear (and wash at night), another to put on after my end-of-the-day shower, and the third for when I'm too lazy to wash the worn pair at night.

A third pair can also serve as an emergency replacement. I once miscalculated and squatted too close to some dry weeds that attached what seemed like a hundred burrs to the inside of my undies, requiring me to change them on the spot and throw them away (later), because removing a hundred burrs from one's undies is impossible, embarrassing, annoying, ridiculous, and time-consuming.

The most comfortable underpants are breathable, lightweight, and made of a fabric that wicks away moisture.

Bras

I once saw Barbra Streisand being interviewed by Ellen DeGeneres on television. Ms. Streisand told Ellen that she was not wearing a bra. To prove it, she encouraged Ellen to slide her hand across her back. Ellen blushed and slid. Apparently, it was true: under Barbra Streisand's black top, there was no bra.

Every woman knows the feeling of liberty that comes with releasing "the girls" at the end of the day. So why not free the girls on the Camino? I do. I don't run the Camino, I walk it, so there's no bouncing to worry about. And the less restrictive my clothing—including undergarments—the more comfortable I feel. I wear a black T-shirt or turtleneck for my inner layer. When it's warm, I skip the inner layer and wear a shirt with two chest pockets: Voilà! No visible nipples.

If you're uncomfortable going without a bra, consider wearing a sports bra. Some styles of sports bras are less constricting than traditional brassieres, and with a pullover and/or T-back style, you won't have to worry about falling-down straps. The fabric often has wicking properties, too.

Let's get started on how the layering system works for your Camino clothing.

Layer 1: Inner Layer

the clothing closest to your skin, not including undergarments—worn for extra warmth or for sleeping

Personal preference determines whether the top half of your inner layer is a long-underwear top or a regular shirt that is long-sleeve, short-sleeve, crew-neck, or a turtleneck. If it's cold enough, a long-underwear bottom would also be part of your inner layer.

Fall or spring can bring snowflakes and wintery winds to the Camino. An inner layer provides insulation against these cold conditions. At night, the inner layer can also double as pajamas; you might sleep in a T-shirt and long underwear, for example.

Make sure your inner-layer garments wick moisture away from your body. Again, one can get hot while backpacking even when it's cold. If perspiration clings to your body, you'll feel cold and wet.

T-shirts and Turtlenecks

Generally, I recommend two T-shirts: one long-sleeve and one short-sleeve. But for pilgrimage walks in early spring or late autumn, when there are likely to be hints of winter weather, I'd recommend taking a T-shirt and a long-sleeve turtleneck.

Like many pilgrims, I use one T-shirt for sleeping and reserve the other for walking. When it's really cold, I use both for extra warmth. A long-sleeve T-shirt in a larger-than-usual size can make the layering more comfortable.

Avoid wearing cotton T-shirts on the Camino: the fabric is too heavy and takes too long to dry, and it won't wick away your perspiration. I prefer relatively inexpensive and easy-to-wash polyester T-shirts. Other fabrics also have wicking qualities, and T-shirts are even available in natural fibers such as silk or merino wool (see Fabrics for Outdoor Clothing and Gear in Chapter 14: Shopping Advice).

Long-Underwear Bottoms

I met a French woman on the Camino who wore pantyhose under her hiking pants to keep warm. It's a good idea: you can't find a lighter-weight option than that. For comfort and versatility, however, I take a pair of lightweight long underwear (sometimes called thermal underwear). They come in handy in various situations:

- They keep you warm under your hiking pants and/or rain pants in frigid temperatures.
- They make excellent pajama bottoms on cold nights.
- They can be worn while washing your hiking pants if you don't have an extra pair of pants, or want to wash two pairs of pants, or don't want to wear rain pants while laundering.
- They're a comfortable choice when you want to stretch out to rest on a refuge bunk bed or hang out in the common area.

Another layering option for ultra-light backpackers, although less comfortable, is to wear two pairs of pants (the second pair being your alternate pair of pants) when it's very cold. Make sure one pair is large enough to fit over the other pair.

Layer 2: Mid-Layer

the clothing worn every day on the Camino

Many pilgrims wear a pair of pants and a long-sleeve shirt in mild weather.

Some pilgrims prefer a short-sleeve shirt or a T-shirt, but long sleeves provide better sun protection, as well as just enough warmth when it's not cold enough to wear a fleece or rain jacket.

Wear loose-fitting clothing for good ventilation and comfort. Get the best quality your budget allows: daily use and frequent washings will take a toll on your mid-layer Camino clothes.

Long-Sleeve Shirt

I prefer a classic button-down-style shirt—and I've noticed that so do many other pilgrims on the Camino. The shirt has the following features:

- **A tail.** When untucked, the tail hides a money belt worn outside the pants, against the back, which is more comfortable than wearing it hidden inside the pants, either in front or in back.
- **Long sleeves.** The sleeves provide protection from the sun and some warmth on mild days when adding other layers would be too much. Remember, sleeves can always be rolled up when it's warm.
- **Two chest pockets.** As a woman, I like these pockets because they cover the chest so I feel comfortable not wearing a bra. The pockets are also useful to carry map and guidebook pages needed for the day's walk. And a pair of eyeglasses. And a small memo pad and pen. And a mobile phone.

I'm not the only bulging-pocketed pilgrim: an American I met on the Camino called his shirt's chest pockets "the office."

Look for quick-drying fabric and a design that includes mesh vents under the arms. Some shirts have vents in the back, but those aren't necessarily that helpful while you're carrying a backpack.

Hiking Pants

It's worth investing in hiking pants that are made from a high-tech fabric that's easy to wash and quick drying. That's because you'll wear them every day, perhaps for weeks. Remember that natural fabrics like cotton take too long to dry and weigh too much. And for comfort, baggy is best.

I prefer hiking pants with cargo pockets on the sides that can hold the things I want access to while walking during the day: sunglasses, a bandana, tissues, a pocket-size camera, lip balm, chewing gum, a tube of sunscreen, and a wallet and/or coin purse with cash for the day's expenses.

Many pilgrims wear cargo-style convertible hiking pants, which can be converted into shorts or capris with a quick zip around the pant leg.

CONVERTIBLE PANTS FOR WOMEN (L) AND MEN (R): ZIP OFF THE LEG BOTTOMS TO MAKE SHORTS
(PILGRIM COUPLE ON THE VÉZELAY ROUTE)

Most pilgrims take two pairs of pants. One is for daily use and the second pair can be worn . . .

- as "evening dress" for dining out and/or sightseeing;
- after showering at the end of the day's walk;
- as "plan B" pants on those days when mud covers the lower legs of your main pants and there isn't time to wash them (convertible pants are handy in this situation—just unzip and wash the bottoms); and
- for variety, when you get sick of wearing the same pants every day for weeks.

Note that the weight of hiking pants varies, depending on features and fabrics. Weigh the choices and choose the lightest— especially for that extra pair, which you'll usually be carrying in your backpack.

Taking Only One Pair of Hiking Pants

A case could be made that the second pair of pants is not really essential, and fits into the nice-to-have category.

Some minimalist backpackers use their rain pants or long underwear as a second pair of pants, getting multiple uses out of what's already in their backpack.

I've tried that, but found long underwear or rain pants uncomfortable for evening wear—especially in hot weather. Another issue with rain pants is that it's possible to wear off the waterproof coating on the fabric from so much use.

I compromise by taking capris as my second pair of pants. Capris usually weigh less than the typical hiking pant because they're shorter in length with minimal features. Women may be more familiar with the capri style than men, but capris can be found for men too.

Layer 3: Insulation Layer

for added warmth, both day and night

The insulation layer can be worn while backpacking when the physical activity—and your rain gear, if it's raining—isn't enough to keep you warm. It can also be used in the evening while resting in your accommodations or going out to eat and to see the local sights.

Wool sweaters or jumpers are not recommended: they're bulky and weigh too much when carried in the backpack. Instead, consider choosing one of the following insulation garments typically worn by pilgrims on the Camino.

Fleece

Most pilgrims wear a fleece pullover or a zippered fleece jacket. Lightweight (lighter than wool) and fast drying, fleece is a warm insulation layer.

The choices are numerous: my outdoor-gear co-op offers more than 500 fleece jackets or pullovers on their website. Choose wisely, however: many of these are irresistibly cuddly but too bulky and heavy for a Camino backpack. A 100-weight fleece is usually sufficient for most people to use while hiking.

Choose a lightweight fleece fabric, with the fewest features you can find. A fleece pullover will likely weigh less than a fleece jacket because it has just a short zipper or none at all. The pullover style may also come without pockets. Again, less material always means less weight. Some fleece jackets use a laminate to provide more insulation than the heavier fleeces provide. But a caution: that insulation might diminish breathability.

Down Vest

I prefer to use a down vest as my insulation layer on the Camino. A vest covering my torso feels nearly as warm as a fleece or down-filled jacket, but since it's sleeveless it's not as bulky. If my arms feel cold, I add layers: a long-sleeve T-shirt under a long-sleeve hiking shirt, combined with a rain jacket over the vest, has always provided enough warmth for me on the Camino.

Backpackers like down fill because it provides the greatest warmth for the lightest weight. It's also highly compressible. My vest weighs 198 grams (7 ounces) and fits in a stuff sack slightly larger than my two fists put together.

The drawback of down fill is that it loses its insulating properties when it gets wet. Thus, I make sure to cover my down vest with a waterproof jacket or a poncho when it's raining. I also try to avoid overheating while wearing the down vest under the jacket, either by taking frequent breaks or by removing the vest as soon as I feel hot. That's because excessive perspiration can also get the down vest wet.

Find a down vest without pockets, or only two hand pockets without zippers, to keep its weight down.

If down fill is too expensive for your budget, consider a vest filled with synthetic fiber. Some synthetic fills have nearly the same warmth-to-weight ratio as down fill.

Pullover Puff Jacket

If you think you'd miss sleeves by using a vest, another lightweight insulation-layer option is a pullover jacket with down or synthetic fill, often called a "puff" jacket. I saw a pullover puff jacket online that weighed 255 grams (9 ounces). It stuffed into one of its own pockets.

Cold-Weather Clothing

Wintry weather can appear early in the fall, or persist until late in the spring. If you're walking during these shoulder months, plan to bring a few extra things for cold weather—or plan for ways to stay warm using what's already in your backpack.

You can always mail winter gear home, or give it away, when warmer temperatures appear on your journey. Conversely, you can buy what you need along the Camino if winter arrives early.

Walking in Winter

I strongly recommend not walking the Camino in the winter months, particularly if you're a novice backpacker.

It's tempting to time your trip to avoid the pilgrim crowds—especially on the most popular route, the Camino Francés, where refuge beds are occasionally in short supply from late spring through early fall. However, many pilgrims' accommodations close in the winter, as do some restaurants and bar-cafés. Also, the days are shorter, and it's difficult to see trail markers or navigate rough trails in the dark. Some Camino walking stages—the distances between accommodations—would be impossible to accomplish within daylight hours in the winter months.

Even a devout loner could find a winter's walk too lonely. There's a safety factor, too: few, if any, pilgrims will be walking behind you in case you need help. Winter's weather can be tough, even dangerous.

Creative Warmth

When surprised by cold weather, use what's already in your backpack:

- Wear long underwear under your hiking pants for warmth. When it's extremely cold, wear long underwear, hiking pants, *and* rain pants.
- Wear a short-sleeve T-shirt over a long-sleeve T-shirt (or turtleneck). You could also do the opposite—wear the long-sleeve T-shirt over the short-sleeve. But even though you'll get warmer after hiking some distance, you might still appreciate the long-sleeve T-shirt covering your arms when it's cold. Wearing the short-sleeve shirt over the long-sleeve shirt keeps you from having to take off both shirts in the cold air (to remove the short-sleeve shirt underneath and wear just the long-sleeve). When it's extremely cold, wear both T-shirts under your hiking shirt along with your insulation and outer layers.
- Use a jacket or poncho hood over a hat to keep your head warm.
- Let extra-long sleeves cover cold hands.
- Use a spare pair of socks, such as your sleeping socks, as mittens; cover them with plastic bags or waterproof stuff sacks if it's raining.
- Use safety pins to pin together a pair of socks for an emergency ear band. This one is guaranteed to make others smile.

Your fleece, vest, or other insulating garment is the thickest layer between you and the cold. Starting in early spring? Choose an appropriately warm insulation garment, and mail it home once temperatures rise. Replace it with a lighter insulation layer to handle unseasonably cool weather or potentially cold higher elevations. Ending in late autumn? Buy, or have someone mail to you, a warmer insulation layer—and perhaps a rain jacket to replace a poncho.

Carrying a Few Extra Items for Warmth

The hands, head, and ears are most vulnerable to cold. If you tend to get cold easily, you might consider carrying a few items to provide extra protection.

Gloves

Fleece gloves are warm and often the most lightweight option, but they're not waterproof. If you're using a walking stick, at least one hand will get wet if it's raining. And if you use two walking poles, both hands will get wet.

An ultralight backpacker might keep gloves from getting wet by abducting waterproof stuff sacks from their original use in the backpack, or using ordinary plastic bags, to cover the fleece gloves.

If not using a walking stick or walking poles, you can hide fleece-gloved hands under the extra-long sleeves of a waterproof jacket.

Or, take lightweight waterproof gloves. If your hands tend to feel cold, take liners for warmth.

Fleece Ear Band

This is my favorite cold-weather item. It weighs almost nothing and, combined with a hat and a hood, makes a big difference in keeping the head and ears warm.

An ear band doesn't contribute to overheating while walking, either, like beanie- or Sherpa-style hats sometimes do.

Scarf

Weigh your favorite winter scarf; its total weight may surprise you.

Instead of a scarf, consider using an all-purpose bandana to cover your face like a bandit—over the nose, falling below the chin—when it suddenly gets cold.

I've used this approach while walking in below-freezing temperatures on the Camino, and the thin cotton bandana provided perfect cover for my nose, chin, and cheeks.

Cold-Weather Hats

There are several good options for a warm hat, such as a lightweight merino wool or fleece beanie style. Fleece or merino wool Sherpa-style hats, with their drop-down earflaps, keep both the ears and the head warm.

Those who are extremely sensitive to cold temperatures might try a balaclava, which pulls over the head to cover the head, neck, and the lower part of the face.

And there are other hats to consider too—for hot days, rainy days, or perfect-weather days.

Hats

DEAD STRAW HAT ALONG THE VÍA DE LA PLATA ROUTE, SPAIN

Ditch vanity, sentimentality, or romantic notions when choosing a hat for the Camino. Think *practicality*.

All right, I confess. I know this now because I once let vanity and sentimentality overrule practicality. It was my first pilgrimage (the one where I carried too many fears in my backpack).

I wanted to remember a deceased friend by wearing her beloved black beret on the Camino. And a mirror at home suggested I looked slightly charming, maybe a bit bohemian, in that black beret.

I started walking the Camino in Roncesvalles, a Basque village in the Spanish Pyrenees. As I passed through other Basque villages and towns, it became clear that practically every Basque man with a little gray in his hair wore a black beret.

Along the way I learned that the French word *béret* means "Basque cap." The black beret is a symbol of solidarity, pride, and tradition, especially among Basque men of a certain age. Not only did I feel ridiculous, but the beret was useless in the rain and provided little warmth. I mailed it home and started wearing my plan-B hat: a baseball hat.

BASQUE MAN WEARING A BLACK BERET IN PAMPLONA, SPAIN, ALONG THE CAMINO FRANCÉS ROUTE

Camino Hats: A Personal Matter

Telling someone to wear a particular hat is almost like telling someone to wear a particular type of underpants. It's personal. I'll share my opinions and experiences on the matter of hats, but you'll have to decide what's best for you.

Here's my hat strategy: I take two. I take a bucket hat to cover my head when it's hot, and a baseball hat for mild to cold weather.

Spring or autumn on the Camino can be both freezing cold *and* extremely hot—sometimes changing from one day to the next. Summer is typically hot, but it can also turn rainy and cold. That's why it's practical to carry a couple of hat choices.

Baseball-Style Hat

Although a baseball-style hat is not a warm hat, it has one great advantage: When it's cold, but not terribly so, I cover the baseball hat with the hood of my rain jacket or poncho. The hat's stiff bill holds the hood away from my face so it doesn't obstruct my view or diminish my ability to hear—especially when it's raining.

I take a *waterproof* baseball hat. My first one wasn't waterproof, and the bill got wet even when covered by a hood. The wetness soaked from the bill into the sweatband and beyond, leaving me with a soggy hat and a cold forehead.

As already mentioned, when it's extremely cold I might wear a fleece ear band—usually under the baseball hat. But when it's windy and cold, I'll wear the fleece band *over* the hat to lock it down. (I meant it when I said there's no room for vanity on the Camino!)

I've also worn a fleece Sherpa-style hat under the baseball hat in cold weather. It's essential to choose an adjustable baseball hat, so you can expand the hat's diameter to fit over the thickness of an ear band or a Sherpa- or beanie-style hat.

Bucket Hat

For sun protection on hot days, I use a bucket hat. It is sometimes called a fisherman's hat, although this varies by culture. Do a search for "bucket hat" in Google Images and you'll see the kind I'm talking about.

A bucket hat is typically made in a lightweight cotton fabric and has a short- to medium-size brim. Some might prefer a wider-brimmed hat, but be aware that wide brims can be annoying when walking in sunny but windy conditions. While a chinstrap might keep the hat from blowing away across the landscape, a constantly flopping brim is irritating.

I've found the bucket hat to be the lightest-weight option for a sun hat. It's also the most resistant to abuse: I stuff it in my backpack or a pocket without worrying about it losing its shape. It has a thin chinstrap too.

On extremely hot days I might soak the bucket hat under a village fountain, or pour water into the hat from a water bottle, and put the hat on my head again for sweet relief from the heat.

Vanity Again: A Hot Hat Story

Here's another hat-choice mistake I once made.

I planned to start walking on the Vía de la Plata route near Seville, in southern Spain, in seriously hot temperatures during the early weeks of September. Seville is called the "frying pan of Europe" because of its heat.

I thought my bucket hat would provide inadequate shade, and besides, a stylish hat seduced me. It spoke to me of safaris and other romantic outdoor adventures, and although it was expensive, I bought it.

But it failed to perform in the frying pan. Air didn't flow through the mesh fabric in the crown of the hat as promised. The velour-like sweatband inside cooked my head. Although the wide brim provided shade, it made the hat feel heavy. I frequently had to take the hat off just to cool down, even under the blazing sun. And the slightest breeze made the brim flop up and down before my eyes.

My walking partner had also bought a hat from this famous hat company. Hers was a different model, with a more understated style and a shorter brim. She loved it. The hat felt light on her head. The sweatband was made of a light fabric, and grommets allowed airflow in the crown. It was practical—and worse still, it looked cute.

I sacked my horrid hat after I found a paper hat for €6 in a town along the Camino. Yes, a 100 percent paper hat. It was cool as could be, and it held on in the wind—even without a chinstrap.

A paper hat is useless in the rain, of course, and it was quickly squashed to shapelessness in my backpack—it wasn't really a practical Camino hat—but my waterproof baseball-style hat still waited quietly in my pack, ready for serious duty.

So for a time, in roasting temperatures under the intense Spanish sun, the paper hat was perfect.

Maybe it was kind of cute, too.

We've looked at the clothing layers that can help you stay comfortable in most situations on your pilgrimage; now let's look at ways to stay dry on the Camino. This will be your "outer shell"—the fourth and final layer of clothing to consider when planning what to wear on a Camino pilgrimage.

CHAPTER 4

CAMINO RAIN GEAR
Planning for the Worst-Case Rainstorm Scenario

Layer 4: Outer Shell

provides protection, primarily from wind and rain as well as snow, which is also possible on early-spring or late-autumn pilgrimages

Imagine walking in a steady rain for five hours or more. It's entirely possible you'll have to do this at some point on the Camino, where it takes that long to walk a typical day's twenty-plus kilometers.

Plan for the worst, even in summer. If you're walking to Santiago, you'll be passing through Galicia, a lush green paradise with abundant rain all year long. But a pilgrim can face rainstorms anywhere, even on the driest plains of Spain. The French routes cross luscious green landscapes, a clue that you can expect rain there as well.

In short, rain gear is a must for the Camino, and it's important to choose wisely.

Umbrella?

Imagine holding an umbrella aloft for four or five hours, perhaps while using a walking stick. Then add strong winds.

Clearly, an umbrella is not a good choice for a Camino pilgrim.

Poncho Versus Rain Jacket

Pilgrims typically use a rain poncho or a rain jacket. I've worn both on the Camino, and both have their pros and cons. Ultimately, which to use is a matter of personal preference.

Sometimes one's preference comes about through experience. One year I began walking the French Le Puy route on April 1, a day that was all blue skies and warm sunshine—until the weather suddenly got mad. During the following eight days, my fellow pilgrims and I walked, heads down, through a mistral—a cold, relentless day-and-night wind, the kind that justifies the cliché "a howling wind."

The word *mistral* has its roots in the Latin word *magister*, meaning "master." This "master wind" blows from northern Europe through southern France, not relenting until the force scatters upon reaching the Mediterranean. A legend says that an old Napoleonic law pardoned crimes of passion—such as murder—if the violent act occurred during a mistral.

Luckily, I had a rain jacket with me when the mistral kicked up on that Camino journey. Other pilgrims found that their ponchos turned into giant sails, constantly flapping in the outrageous winds. A Swiss woman told me that her poncho was whipped up by the winds and wrapped around her neck. When the rains joined the winds, the poncho was useless.

But one's choice of rain gear need not be strictly either-or; you could use both on one journey. I once mailed a rain jacket home after buying a poncho to wear during warmer days at the end of my journey. You could also do the reverse: when walking from summer into cooler autumn months, ditch the poncho and buy a jacket in France or Spain when you need it.

We'll look at both the benefits and drawbacks of ponchos and rain jackets, and some of the features of each. Then you can decide what might work best for you. First, let's look at the different styles of ponchos, which can vary quite a bit.

Ponchos

Despite the experiences of those poncho-wearing pilgrims who hiked with me during the mistral, I'm not prejudiced against ponchos. They do have their advantages, which I'll explain shortly.

Ponchos come in a range of styles. Some ponchos reach the thighs. Others extend to the knees. Serious ponchos fall all the way to the ankles.

Packing Tips

Many pilgrims specifically recommend the Spanish-made Altus Atmospheric Poncho (you can buy them at www.barrabes.com— click on Barrabes International for language options, including English). This particular poncho has a pouch-like space at the back to cover a backpack, but you can also make an adjustment to cinch that bulky part when you're not carrying a backpack.

Depending on how tall you are, and the size you get (they come in two sizes), the length drops below the knees to cover the legs to mid-calf or to just above the ankles. That length helps to prevent the poncho from severely flapping or billowing in strong winds. Although the Altus is not made with a breathable fabric, there is some venting that occurs through design features, and hopefully from the bagginess of the poncho itself. There are some drawbacks to any poncho design like this: you might feel hot while hiking during rainy but warm weather, and it might not feel warm enough when it's cold and windy but not raining.

One poncho style even provides a pouch-like space at the back to allow room for the bulk of a backpack. Look for back-panel snaps if you choose this style; that way you'll have less bagginess behind you while wearing it without a backpack. Most backpacking ponchos, however, are simply longer in the back to allow the poncho to cover a backpack and fall to the back of the legs at about equal length to the poncho's front. It's a good idea to check the length of the poncho when you're not wearing a backpack to be sure it's not so long in the back that it might cause you to trip.

Some poncho hoods have a short bill, along with a drawcord, to help the hiker maintain some degree of peripheral vision. Many poncho hoods only have a cord to cinch the hood tighter around the head. In that case, hikers often wear a waterproof hat with a bill underneath the hood to improve their vision.

Poncho sleeves also vary. Some are short and narrow in width, with the length falling to the mid-upper arm. If you're wearing a long-sleeve shirt, this is not a great option: your shirt's sleeves will get wet. If you roll up your shirtsleeves, your arms might feel cold.

Most ponchos I've used, or have seen other pilgrims use, have formless sleeves. A snap secures the fabric underneath the arms to provide a sleeve-type structure. In this case the length covering the arms will vary depending on the poncho size and the length of your arms.

Whatever poncho style or model you choose, keep in mind the goal: the best rain protection for the least weight.

Poncho Benefits

Ponchos are popular with pilgrims because they're lightweight, use little space in the backpack, and cover both the body and the backpack. Quick to throw on when the rain begins and quick to take off when the rain stops, they're perfect for intermittent showers. And because ponchos are so baggy, they provide more ventilation than a zipped-up rain jacket.

A unique benefit for women: a poncho is like a personal tent, making bathroom breaks easy. Use a tree or a large rock to help keep your balance, and you won't have to take off your backpack and poncho in the pouring rain. A poncho can provide the same cover when it's not raining—especially handy on the barren plains in Spain or on a part of the Camino that is crowded with other pilgrims.

Poncho Drawbacks

Ponchos do have some disadvantages, however. Perhaps the most difficult challenge is when strong winds turn the poncho into a flapping sail, exposing your body and backpack to the rain. Some backpackers tie a cord around their waist to hold the poncho in place, though the material hanging below that tie could still be whipped up by the winds. Whether it's windy or not, lower arms are exposed through the baggy arm holes of a poncho, making it likely that the sleeves of your shirt (and your watch) will get wet.

Another drawback, although perhaps how much of a problem this is depends on when you walk the Camino, is that the thin poncho material and baggy fit mean that ponchos are not much help in keeping you warm. You could need extra layers underneath when it's cold. A poncho is not a lightweight option after all if you need to carry heavier clothing to wear underneath the poncho for cold days or nights.

Finally, a wet poncho is a big and awkward thing to deal with. It's best to spread it out to dry at the end of the day, but there's usually limited personal space in pilgrims' refuges.

Essential Poncho Features

- 100 percent waterproof fabric (avoid "water resistant"!)
- fully taped (sealed) seams
- snaps on bottom hem to diminish that billowy effect in the wind
- snaps underneath the arms if the arms are not a defined fit
- a hood that cinches with a cord
- a bill on the hood if you don't have a waterproof hat with a bill to wear underneath

Now let's compare a rain jacket to a poncho. By doing this we'll also see the benefits and drawbacks of wearing a jacket.

Rain-Jacket Benefits (Compared to a Poncho)

- warmer, due to closer fit that helps retain body heat
- better performance in the wind

- more comfortable and versatile for evening wear on the Camino
- more comfortable and versatile before and after the Camino journey (when visiting European friends, sightseeing)
- easier to hang for drying
- no worry about a wristwatch or sleeves getting wet

Rain-Jacket Drawbacks (Compared to a Poncho)

- warmer (though if you get a larger-size jacket it could mimic a poncho's bagginess/ventilation, which would make it less warm)
- heavier (depending on jacket features)
- doesn't cover a backpack (more later on ways to overcome this drawback)

Rain Jackets: Essential Features

If you decide to take a rain jacket rather than a poncho on the Camino, here are some important features to consider when choosing that rain jacket.

Your rain jacket absolutely must be both waterproof and breathable—even though the fabric technologies used to create that combination are sometimes imperfect. Grime on the surface of the jacket fabric, for example, can diminish the effectiveness of the waterproof fabric and could allow water to seep into the fabric.

Another (less preventable) imperfection of waterproof-breathable fabric becomes apparent when high humidity levels in the air coincide with high levels of exertion on the trail. This combination can overwhelm the fabric's ability to breathe, and you can get wet inside the jacket from your own perspiration.

Rain Jacket "Fail"

I once crossed the French Pyrenees (high level of exertion) while it was raining (high humidity levels). I wore a jacket that was made by a respected outdoor-gear company. The photo that advertised the jacket showed a man standing under a waterfall—implying "waterproof"! But, even though it was raining only moderately that day in the Pyrenees, I felt chilled and wet, as though my rain jacket had completely lost its waterproof quality. The problem was really caused by the combination of high-level exertion and a high humidity level—the jacket fabric simply couldn't breathe. So I wasn't wet from the rain, but from my own perspiration.

In other circumstances, that lightweight waterproof and breathable jacket worked well. Unfortunately, the technology to make a perfect waterproof and breathable fabric that works all the time doesn't yet exist. But you're more likely to stay comfortable and dry—most of the time—with a jacket that is waterproof and breathable.

Other jacket-fabric choices, such as waterproof but not breathable, or a fabric that is water resistant rather than waterproof (read garment labels carefully!), will be less effective. Water-resistant fabric is for light rain only; water will quickly penetrate it in a downpour. Again: look for waterproof. You want to be able to wear the jacket in the rain for hours—a not-uncommon situation faced on the Camino, unfortunately—without getting wet!

This highlights a key difference between ponchos and jackets: waterproof but not-breathable fabric is fine for ponchos. Their ventilation is in their bagginess, which makes it less likely that condensation will form inside the poncho.

More Rain-Jacket Features to Consider

Lightweight construction. To determine the weight of a jacket, read product specifications when shopping online or ask the clerk in a store to weigh it for you. Your insulation layer, like a fleece jacket, will keep you warm. The jacket is a shell to protect you from wind and precipitation. Get a lightweight jacket.

Full-zip jacket. It's easier to put on and take off than an anorak (pullover) style. One can also unzip the jacket to cool off.

Larger size. A larger size allows for more ventilation and space for layering. The longer sleeves can cover hands to keep them warm and dry.

Jacket length. For complete coverage, choose a jacket that falls below the waist of your rain pants.

Hood. Look for a stiff bill that keeps the hood from collapsing around your face and making peripheral vision difficult. I also use a rainproof baseball-style hat underneath the hood to further improve my vision and to provide cover for my old-lady reading glasses when it's raining and I need to check the map or route guide.

Fully taped (sealed) seams. Make sure *all* jacket seams are taped. Some jackets have "critically taped seams," which means only the most exposed seams are protected.

Zipper flaps. These prevent water from seeping in between the zipper's teeth. To save weight, look for a zipper that is itself fully sealed to prevent leaks, rather than being covered with a flap.

Storm flaps. Pockets with flaps are less likely to leak.

Vents. Since they're often found under the arms, these vents are sometimes called "pit zips." Zippers and flaps add weight, but if you tend to overheat it's worth considering pit zips. Otherwise, a larger-size jacket may be the better option for ventilation.

Two-way zipper. An option to unzip from the bottom and/or the top of the jacket provides more ventilation. Velcro or snaps on a flap outside the zipper also offer more ventilation options, but remember that these features add weight to a jacket because of the extra materials used.

Face guard. A high front collar protects the lower part of your face from cold winds and rain.

Adjustable hood and cuffs. Additional warmth or ventilation can be achieved by adjusting the hood and cuffs of a jacket.

Pockets. Two are sufficient. The more pockets, the more weight.

Keeping Your Legs Dry

While backpacking in New Zealand some years ago, I noticed that many Kiwis (as New Zealanders often call themselves) wore shorts under their rain ponchos. The idea was to stay cool while hiking and to avoid wet pant legs by eliminating the pants.

But when I tried the shorts-under-poncho method my legs felt numb in the cold. I also had to avoid rest breaks, as the inactivity made my bare legs feel even colder. In addition, the top of my socks got wet and that wetness soaked into my boots. Blisters-to-be love that moisture. So I returned to a combo of poncho and rain pants.

The idea of wearing shorts under a poncho or a jacket can still be tempting in warm temperatures, and the wet-socks problem could be solved by wearing gaiters (more on these in a minute). Still, spring and fall weather and high elevations can turn too wet and cold for my cowardly legs. And even Camino summers can bring cool temperatures.

If you have Kiwi rather than cowardly legs, try the poncho-shorts-gaiters combo. But try this at home first, in the cold. It's best to feel confident in your gear before your Camino journey is underway.

If this combination doesn't seem right for you, consider rain pants or rain chaps.

Rain Pants

Avoid "rubber pants."

That's what one pilgrim called her rain pants. They were waterproof, but *not breathable*. They kept the rain out, but kept in the perspiration. The consequence? Wet, clammy legs.

Get lightweight, breathable rain pants. Again, the key word is *breathable*.

Find a rain-pant style that has zippers (some rain pants use Velcro) on the sides of the legs so you can quickly pull them on over your footwear and hiking pants. You'll appreciate that feature on days with intermittent rain showers, when the rain gear goes on, comes off, goes on, comes off . . .

41

Rain Chaps

Not familiar with rain chaps? Think of a cowboy on his horse, rustling up cattle and wearing leather coverings over his blue jeans. Those are chaps.

Rain chaps consist of two separate fully enclosed leg coverings—basically, two pant legs. Typically, each leg is secured to the hiking pants with a cord that ties to a belt loop. They're quick to pull on over hiking pants and footwear. The advantage: they provide a bit more ventilation than rain pants.

Baggy is best, for that good ventilation—and to fit over footwear.

If you use chaps it's essential to have a poncho or rain jacket that's long enough to protect the exposed inner thigh and your rear end and keep your hiking pants from getting wet. The distinctive cut of rain chaps doesn't cover these areas.

Gear Guide

Rain chaps are difficult to find, so I once made a pair. First, I sketched out a pattern on butcher paper. Then I cut and sewed waterproof fabric according to the pattern.

But it turned out the fabric was only water resistant, not waterproof. The homemade chaps worked fine in light rains, but they failed in an hours-long downpour one day. I got soaked and had to buy a pair of rain pants at the next town along the Camino route.

If rain chaps appeal to you but you can't find them, consider making your own. I'm not a seamstress, but I found them quite easy to make. Just make sure to verify that the fabric is *waterproof.*

Gaiters

Want to try that Kiwi poncho-shorts combo? Consider taking gaiters to keep the top of your socks dry.

I've never worn gaiters, but I can imagine their practicality in many situations:

- They prevent small stones from sneaking into your footwear—especially footwear that doesn't cover the ankles, like hiking shoes.

- They'll help you stay dry when walking in taller weeds or grasses that are wet with morning dew.
- As part of a rain-gear system, gaiters could fill the gap between the hem of an almost-ankle-length poncho and the top of your footwear.
- They're easier to wash than rain pants or hiking pants, so it would be useful to wear gaiters over pants or below shorts on a fine day when the trail is still muddy from rainstorms. If you're wearing hiking shoes, rather than ankle-high boots, gaiters would be particularly helpful in mud.

Rain-Gear Care

A fabric-coating substance, durable water repellent (DWR), is applied to the outside of a fabric to make water bead up and roll off. Over time, that DWR could be scraped off the fabric. Dirt or grime can also reduce DWR's effectiveness.

Thus, it's a good idea to keep rain gear in a separate bag. Then the bag—instead of the jacket, poncho, rain pants, chaps, or gaiters—gets scraped when going in and out of the backpack. I've found that the lightweight cellophane bag that a new rain jacket arrived in works perfectly as protection for the DWR coating.

Test older rain jackets, ponchos, and rain pants in the shower before taking them with you. If they've lost their ability to repel water, better to discover that at home than on the Camino.

If you find that a garment is no longer waterproof, you can use a spray to restore the DWR protection. Dry cleaners sometimes offer a service to restore DWR protection. (Give the garment another good test after either of these treatments.)

Follow provided instructions to clean waterproof garments—they sometimes recommend soaps to use—or *not* use. Sometimes the instructions indicate you should dry the garment in a dryer; others insist you should hang the garment to dry in the open air. Some instructions suggest you could restore some of the DWR properties yourself by pressing a warm or hot iron to the fabric.

Now that we've explored the options for staying dry, let's tackle another very important issue for Camino pilgrims: footwear.

CHAPTER 5

CAMINO FOOTWEAR
Including Socks and Alternate Footwear

A Frenchwoman insisted that her high-tech running shoes were the best shoes for the Camino.

A Spanish man pointed to his battered department-store sneakers and said, "These are the shoes you must wear for the Camino."

An American woman said wearing sport sandals with socks was the only way to walk the Camino.

A Basque man said his trail-hiking shoes were an excellent choice for the Camino journey.

A Frenchman who's walked *thousands* of kilometers on Camino routes—both popular and obscure—always wears hiking boots. His wife even mails him a replacement pair when his boots no longer offer sufficient tread or support during his lengthy journeys.

I always wear boots too.

These photos, which I took on the Vézelay route in France, illustrate one reason why I wear boots.

WHY BOOTS, EXHIBIT A: CAMINO MUD ON TRAIL

WHY BOOTS, EXHIBIT B: CAMINO MUD ON ME

(Note: I found that these boots were too heavy and stiff for the Camino. I've since changed to a more flexible, lightweight boot.)

My Case for Wearing Boots

- I prefer covered ankles when walking on muddy trails.
- I want support for my feet and ankles when walking on steep, slippery, or rocky trails.
- I like keeping my feet dry in rain (and perhaps snow) and when crossing the occasional creek.
- Ankle-high boots diminish the chance that tiny pebbles from the trail will sneak into my footwear. Sandals or shoes provide easier access for these pests.
- Ankle-high boots, covered by rain pants, keep my socks dry. If you wear shoes, your socks could get wet at the ankles while you walk, even if they're covered by rain pants.

...And My Favored Boot Type

I've experimented with mountaineering-style boots that have a sturdy body and a thick sole. But Camino routes often follow country lanes and roads, and I've found that boots that are too heavy and stiff make my feet ache after walking long distances on tarmac. I've heard other pilgrims offer the same complaint.

Lightweight boots, made with a combination of fabric and leather, have enough sole and flexibility to endure a variety of Camino surfaces. Being lightweight, they're also easier to lift with each step.

I've had success with boots made with a Gore-Tex fabric that makes the boots both waterproof and breathable under most conditions. That technology has kept my feet dry, warm in cold weather, and even reasonably cool in hot weather.

Choosing What's Best for You

While I make the case for boots, others will just as emphatically make their case for sport sandals, hiking shoes, running shoes, or an old pair of skimpy sneakers.

Pilgrim Stories

I once tried a pair of lightweight hiking shoes for a Camino journey. They were not waterproof (I'm embarrassed to say!). Day one: fine. Day two: I walked on a grassy trail covered with an early-morning dew. My feet got wet, and within an hour I had huge blisters on the bottoms of my feet that took days to heal. I had to buy other footwear in France—and break it in on the Camino journey—not the best way to test new footwear.

Choose your Camino footwear based on what you know about your feet—and the rest of your body, as footwear also affects the knees, hips, and back. Also consider these factors:

- When you're going
- The terrain for the route
- The kind of weather you'll likely experience (for example: sandals or sneakers would be uncomfortable during a surprise spring snow, or during hours—or days—of rain)
- How far you'll be walking (several weeks of daily walking will have more impact on your feet than walking for several days)

If you choose to wear light footwear (especially sandals, which don't offer a lot of support) make sure your your backpack is also lightweight—a heavy backpack puts enormous pressure on the feet and ankles.

On all of the Camino routes, the terrain often varies from day to day. To help you decide what footwear will work best for you, here are just a few of the typical situations you'll encounter on nearly all Camino routes.

A DIRT ROAD

A STEEP AND ROCKY TRAIL

A COUNTRY LANE (LOOKS EASY, BUT HOURS OF WALKING ON PAVEMENT, DAY AFTER DAY, IS ACTUALLY QUITE HARD ON THE FEET)

Most Important: Test Your Footwear

Before you leave home, wear your fully loaded backpack while testing your footwear. Do it every day for a few days to test a variety of conditions. Walk in the rain. Walk on muddy trails. Walk on steep, rocky paths. Walk down slippery, muddy hills. Walk for long distances on paved surfaces. If you're headed to Santiago, these are likely the conditions you'll experience.

It's also helpful to break in new footwear by wearing it every day for a few weeks, even when not carrying a backpack.

Pilgrim Stories

An experienced pilgrim fellow I know once bought some fancy new boots in London before heading to France to begin another pilgrimage. Of course, that didn't allow time for testing the boots, and it turned out to be a painful journey: he discovered the heavy boots made his feet swell and pinched and jammed his toes too. To add to his misery, it was a spring season with unusual amounts of rainfall, and the unseasoned boots (not yet fully waterproofed) allowed his feet to get wet, which then led to foot rot—a nasty condition. He completed his journey, but had to pamper his feet back to health long after returning home. It's important for me to repeat: test your footwear before going on a pilgrimage.

Footwear Shopping Tips
Shop Late in the Day

Shop when your feet are warm or, even better, when they're hot. That's how your feet will feel while walking long distances. You'll be more likely to choose appropriately roomy footwear if you shop when your feet are naturally swollen at the end of an active day.

Gear Guide

To ensure you choose footwear that fits well, when you go shopping be sure to wear the socks, footpads, and/or orthotics you plan to use on the Camino.

Buy at a Bricks-and-Mortar Store

It's best to buy footwear in person at a store rather than online. If you choose to shop online, be sure to buy from a company with a liberal exchange policy.

Find a Trained Sales Clerk

Look for a sales clerk that knows how to accurately measure feet, including heel width, forefoot width, and the usual foot-length measurement. These factors might indicate a particular brand or model that will work well for you. Boot and shoe manufacturers are sometimes known for particular characteristics—one company might make boots or shoes that typically have a wide toe box, for example, while another company's products might be known for their narrow heel beds. A knowledgeable sales clerk should be able to quickly steer you toward the appropriate footwear for your foot's size, shape, and structure.

Be Picky

Ultimately, you know what feels best. Test the footwear in the store by walking around for an hour or so.

If possible, go up and down stairs or a steep ramp to see if

- your toes have enough room in the toe box;
- your heel lifts up inside the shoe (it shouldn't lift more than about six millimeters, or a quarter inch); or
- your foot slips inside the boot or shoe when climbing up and down the ramp or stairs (it shouldn't).

See if you can wiggle your toes freely without them rubbing against the inside of the boot or shoe. I met an Australian woman who developed blisters on the baby toe of each foot. Her boots were too short, thus pinching and jamming her toes on every step, especially when going downhill. She quit her journey after two painful days on the Camino.

If you notice even the tiniest friction on the toes or the heel, imagine how your feet will fare walking thousands and thousands of steps with that constant friction.

Avoid Style, Look for Performance

In their design and marketing, almost all footwear companies try to appeal to our fashion sense. Sometimes that's especially true for (their perceptions of) female tastes (pink patches on boots—really?).

Don't let yourself be swayed by color or design. Look for practical footwear that can perform well in a variety of conditions.

That cute pink pattern will likely get covered in mud and cow dung anyway.

Look for a Liberal Exchange Policy

Sometimes you can't know the true character of footwear until you take it out into the world and establish some real intimacy. I once bought a pair of boots that felt perfect in the store. When I started wearing them on short walks to break them in, I became increasingly annoyed by the metal eyelets for the shoestrings. On each step they dug into my foot where it bends. It was clear that the boot design was not suitable for my feet. It was time for a divorce. I restored the newness of the boots by cleaning the sides and bottoms of the soles, and then I returned them for a full refund.

Pilgrim Stories

It's not reasonable to return boots with signs of excessive wear, but sometimes a great store makes exceptions. At the same store that gave me a refund for the eyelets-from-hell boots, I bought a different pair of boots. They passed the critical test walks, and eventually carried me comfortably for the first 480 kilometers (about 300 miles) on the Le Puy route. Then, with about 320 kilometers to go (about 200 miles), I noticed the stitching near the toes starting to unravel on the left boot. Even worse, about the same time I started hearing a squeak in the same left boot—with each step I took. (This constant squeaking can alter one's mental health.) Upon returning home, I took the squeaky, unraveling boot and its twin back to the store. I thought they might just re-stitch the boot. Instead, they gave me a full refund on the well-worn boots that had traveled over 800 kilometers (about 500 miles). I've been a loyal customer ever since, thanks to that generous exchange policy.

Socks
Sock Test

Sock packaging usually prevents us from trying socks on before buying them. Look for a store with a liberal exchange policy, so you can at least unwrap the socks to try them on. A good fit with quality features should be immediately apparent. If not, you can return the socks without any sign of wear.

Sock Shock

Don't be surprised at sock prices. Quality hiking socks are expensive, but they're worth it: today's sock designs, as well as the fabrics used, often help prevent blisters.

However—because socks are so important when backpacking for long distances—the best test is to wear them for several kilometers in the footwear you'll use on the Camino. But then it's only fair to put socks that fail the test walk in a sock drawer for general use, rather than trying to return them.

How Many Pairs of Socks to Take

Ultralight backpackers might take two pairs of socks: one to wear and one to spare. Then they wash the worn pair every night. If the socks are still damp in the morning, the other pair can be worn.

I recommend taking three pairs of hiking socks: one to wear and two to spare. That provides an option to delay the sock-washing chore for a night or two. It also provides an extra pair if you want to change socks midday. Clean, dry socks can also help prevent blisters.

I also take a fourth pair of socks as a luxury item. I wear them after the day's walk, and sleep in them when my feet feel cold. They're baggy and loose so my feet can breathe after their day-long confinement.

Sock Features to Look For
Fit

Look for a sock that fits your foot without any excess material that can bunch, especially at the toes or in the heel. The fit should be snug, yet not so tight as to cut off circulation. A good fit helps to prevent blisters too.

Fabric and Design

Forget cotton socks. They retain moisture and have no wicking quality to pull that moisture away from the skin of your feet. That constant moisture could cause blisters. Cotton socks also take forever to dry.

Many socks today combine synthetic fibers with wool to make the socks less scratchy and more absorbent. This fiber blend also gives them better wicking capabilities. Although wool is not the only choice for sock fabric, many backpackers prefer some type of wool blend because of its cushioning and insulating properties, as well as its durability.

Look for a design without bulging seams. Any nubs of exposed stitching will constantly rub your feet as you walk. That's yet another way to get blisters. Look for flat seams or no seams.

Get socks with reinforced heels and toes. Extra padding under the ball of the foot also helps to cushion your feet.

Liner Socks

The idea of wearing liner socks next to your feet is that this extra layer of material, instead of the skin of your feet, takes the friction inside shoes or boots. They're like a second skin. Liner socks also help wick away moisture. Some liner socks are made of soft merino wool. For people with sensitivities to wool, liner socks in polypropylene, polyester, or silk work well to prevent the outer wool socks from touching the skin.

Some backpackers insist liner socks are essential; others prefer wearing just well-fitting socks with wicking properties.

Experiment: see what works for your feet by trying different options before embarking on your Camino journey.

Sock Care
- Wash socks by hand, inside out, with mild soap.
- Rinse thoroughly—residual soap can irritate the skin.
- Avoid completely drying socks in a hot dryer.
- Hang socks to dry. This helps to prevent any high-tech fabric qualities from breaking down.

Free the Feet: Alternate Footwear

Take another pair of shoes in addition to the ones you'll hike in. It's healthy for your feet to have a break from the footwear you've worn all day while walking.

Since many pilgrims' accommodations require everyone to leave their footwear at the front door, especially if it's wet or covered in mud, you'll want something to wear inside your accommodation for the night.

Your alternate footwear should also be comfortable enough to walk some distance in, since you probably won't want to wear your hiking footwear when you go out to eat or take a stroll in the evenings to sightsee.

Look for the following features for your alternate footwear:

- Adds little to your backpack weight.
- Has enough of a sole to provide comfort and safety on bumpy and uneven cobblestone streets in towns and villages.
- Is waterproof, for use in communal showers.

Flip-flops are a tempting choice because they're so lightweight. If you want to go ultralight, go with flip-flops. Then wear your hiking footwear on evening walks.

IT'S HELPFUL TO CHOOSE ALTERNATE FOOTWEAR THAT ALSO WORKS WELL ON COBBLESTONE STREETS—OTHERWISE TIRED FEET MIGHT HAVE TO STAY CONFINED IN BOOTS WHILE YOU'RE SIGHTSEEING, DINING OUT, OR SHOPPING FOR FOOD AFTER THE LONG DAY'S WALK (STREET IN LIMOGES, FRANCE, ON THE VÉZELAY ROUTE).

Two Suggestions for Alternate Footwear
All-Terrain or Multisport Sandals

All-terrain or multisport sandals are thick-soled sandals that use adjustable straps to hold your foot securely in place. Worn with or without socks, they allow the feet to spread and breathe. If the straps are fabric, instead of leather, this kind of sandal can also be worn in communal showers.

If it's raining in the evening, you could always wear your hiking footwear—unless the weather is warm enough that you won't mind wet feet.

All-terrain sandals also make a great plan-B shoe. If you get serious blisters from your other footwear, and your backpack is not too heavy, these sandals might allow you to continue on your way while letting your blisters heal.

Crocs or Other Rubber Shoes

Yes, they're ugly. But ugly wonderful: they please the feet after hiking all day. I prefer the Crocs model that has several holes on the top and a heel strap.

Disadvantage: feet get wet when it rains.

Advantage: they're great for wearing in communal showers.

Super advantage: rubber shoes weigh less than the durable all-terrain sandals. My beloved Teva sport sandals (both of them together) weigh about 475 grams (just over a pound). The pair of Crocs weighs 252 grams (8.9 ounces).

It's possible to find a sport sandal to rival the weight of the Crocs. I recently found an inexpensive pair of sport sandals that weighed 29 grams (one ounce) less than the Crocs. They're not as durable as my Tevas, but they have a decent-enough sole and they're waterproof.

––––––––––

You should now have a good idea of everything you might want to wear, from head to foot, so let's get started on what Camino pilgrims typically carry in their backpack.

What to
Carry in a Camino
Backpack

CHAPTER 6

SLEEPING BAG OR SHEET?
Choosing Sleeping Gear for the Camino

Sleeping sheets weigh less than sleeping bags, and take up less space in the backpack, which makes them a great choice for a lightweight Camino backpack. But whether they're the best choice is not so straightforward.

Overall, I'd recommend a lightweight sleeping bag as the most practical choice for Camino journeys in both France and Spain, though the reasons are a bit different for each country. I'd also recommend that you visit the Camino pilgrims' forums (they're different, despite the similar website addresses) at www.caminodesantiago.me and www.caminodesantiago.me.uk, where you can post a question about whether to take a sleeping bag or a sleeping sheet on the specific Camino route you want to take. That way you'll get up-to-date information from pilgrims who've recently walked the route.

Gear Guide

Travelers who've slept in youth hostels will be familiar with sleeping sheets, which are often recommended to cover a hostel bed. Sometimes called a travel sheet, it's sized to fit a twin bed and has a large pocket for a pillow. A sleeping-bag liner is a similar option.

Sleeping sheets are typically made of cotton or silk. Cotton costs less, but weighs more than silk. Silk feels luxurious, but it's slippery: blankets covering a silk sheet can slide off during the night (a problem I've experienced firsthand).

Different Routes, Different Sleeping Situations

I'll share my experience on four popular routes in France and Spain to give you an idea of how the sleeping situations on the different routes vary, so you can pack according to your plans.

Spain
On the Camino Francés and Vía de la Plata Routes

On Camino routes in Spain blankets are often not available in the pilgrims' refuges, or they're in short supply.

Some refuges can feel cold at night, even in the summer months. If you can't find a blanket, a sleeping sheet may not be enough to keep you warm.

In remote locations or in small villages with no hotels or inns, a pilgrims' refuge may be the only option for the night's accommodation. This fact, combined with large crowds (common particularly on the Camino Francés), means that beds are not always available in refuges. Sometimes a local school gym or a community center is opened to handle the overflow of pilgrims; pilgrims then sleep on the floor. Sometimes extra mattresses are placed on the floor in a crowded refuge, but even those can become scarce. A sleeping bag is better than a thin sleeping sheet in these situations.

Pilgrim Stories

A friend and her husband walked the Camino Francés route starting in late August, when the temperatures were very hot during the day. They carried sleeping sheets instead of sleeping bags. She admitted that they felt cold on many nights, depending on the type of refuge or its location. Overall, they regretted not having sleeping bags.

France
On the Le Puy and Vézelay Routes

French routes have steadily increased in popularity, so the limited-bed situation that occurs in Spain could also happen on the most traveled pilgrimage routes in France. But for those wanting to take a chance on bringing a sleeping sheet instead of a sleeping bag, it's possible there's a little more flexibility in France. Again, visit the pilgrims' forums to get the latest information.

Le Puy Route. In 2003 I walked the Le Puy route from Le Puy-en-Velay to Saint-Jean-Pied-de-Port, a distance of about 750 kilometers (465 miles). I used a sleeping sheet instead of a sleeping bag. Luckily, I found a blanket and a bed in pilgrims' accommodations for the entire route.

Again, the number of pilgrims walking the Le Puy route has increased since that time, and today I wouldn't have the same confidence that I'd always find a blanket—or even a bed.

Another factor to consider: many of the accommodations on the Le Puy route are not exclusively for Camino pilgrims. Recreational hiking routes and pilgrim routes frequently overlap, so you'll often share these accommodations with weekend and vacation hikers.

Perhaps the key factor in determining whether a sleeping sheet is adequate for the Le Puy route is the time of year you'll be there. Traditional vacation times and French national holidays always bring more hikers and pilgrims to the trails.

Vézelay Route. In the spring of 2006 I walked the Vézelay route, a distance of about 885 kilometers (550 miles), and carried a sleeping bag. That was the first year a comprehensive and updated guidebook was available for the route, and I met only a dozen pilgrims the entire way—until reaching the southernmost portion where it merges with the Le Puy route and two other historic (but less developed) Camino routes. Today, however, the Vézelay route is more popular.

Most of the time I stayed in small inns, bed-and-breakfasts, or hotels. Of course those accommodations had beds with sheets, so I didn't need my sleeping bag. The pilgrim-specific refuges sometimes had as few as four beds, and often those were without blankets. So although I rarely used my sleeping bag on the Vézelay route, I was glad to have it for the several times I really needed it in the pilgrims' refuges. Check the most recently updated Vézelay guidebook (and the pilgrims' forums) for current information on the availability of beds for the Vézelay route.

Ultimately, whether you'll need a sleeping bag on these two popular French routes depends on luck, crowd numbers, where you choose to stay, when you go, and whether blankets are provided and available—which you can't know until you arrive someplace.

That's why, overall, I recommend taking a sleeping bag on the Camino routes in both France and Spain. Then you'll know a warm bed is always with you.

Camping on the Camino

Camping is prohibited on the Camino routes, except in designated camping areas. Check your guidebook: camping facilities, when available, are listed with the other accommodations options.

Choosing a Sleeping Bag

The perfect-for-everyone Camino sleeping bag does not exist. Some suggestions:

- Get the lightest-weight sleeping bag you can find. Look for a sleeping bag that weighs less than a kilogram (about 2 pounds).
- Stuff the bag into the smallest compression sack that will hold it (see Types of Sacks and Bags in Chapter 13: Organizing and Packing Your Backpack). Using a compression sack will diminish the sleeping bag's bulk so it takes up less space inside your backpack.
- Get a sleeping bag designed for moderate temperatures. As a general rule, a sleeping bag that's rated to keep the body warm at 7 degrees Celsius (about 45 degrees Fahrenheit) will keep most pilgrims comfortable at night—even when a pilgrims' refuge lacks heating or air-conditioning (which is not uncommon). But some people tend to feel cold at night, while others tend to sleep warm. Get a sleeping bag with a higher or

lower temperature rating if you think it will be a better match for your sleeping needs.

- If you're planning to walk when the weather is typically hot (late spring, summer, or early fall), consider getting a sleeping bag with a higher temperature rating than "moderate" (in other words, a sleeping bag rated for temperatures above 7 degrees Celsius, or about 45 degrees Fahrenheit). Be aware, however, that it can still get cold in the higher elevations and during storms at any time of the year.
- Down-filled sleeping bags have the best warmth-to-weight ratio, and they also compress the best.
- Synthetic fill also works well, and it's less expensive than a down-fill bag. Advantage for some: many synthetic fills are hypoallergenic.
- A mummy-shape bag, while less roomy for the body, weighs less than a rectangular sleeping bag.

Worried About Feeling Cold at Night?

- Get a sleeping bag designed for below-moderate temperatures, but be mindful of the weight that it will add to your backpack.
- Get down fill: those little feathers are still the best for warmth. Shake the bag at night for maximum fluff to keep you warm. Be sure to have good rain protection for your backpack: down is useless when wet.
- Sleep in long underwear and long-sleeve T-shirt underneath a short-sleeve T-shirt. Wear your insulation layer—a down vest or fleece jacket—when feeling especially cold. In other words: wear everything.
- Bring a mummy bag liner to put inside your sleeping bag for extra warmth (be sure to find a lightweight liner; I've seen some that only weigh about 113 grams, or about four ounces).

Worried About Feeling Too Warm at Night?

- Sleep in a mummy bag liner on top of your sleeping bag (again, look for a liner that weighs only about 113 grams, or about four ounces). If you happen to feel cold later in the night, you can easily climb inside the sleeping bag.

- Plan to sleep in a lightweight short-sleeve T-shirt and your underwear. Most pilgrims do that anyway, and some will do so even if it's cold inside the pilgrims' refuge.
- Finally, a tip that may be obvious but is worth mentioning: if it's too warm, unzip your sleeping bag all the way and arrange it so it covers only part of your body.

Sleeping Pad
Necessity or Luxury?

Some pilgrims take a sleeping pad. It's a good idea if you're worried about the possibility of sleeping on a hard floor during the crowded Camino walking seasons.

Every time I packed for a Camino journey, I considered taking a sleeping pad because I worried about that hard-floor scenario. Then, I'd remember Vidal's words: "We carry our fears in our backpack." So I'd throw away the fear and not take the sleeping pad.

So far, I've never needed it.

But I had the fear once again before walking the Vía de la Plata route. I'd read that the route was increasing in popularity, and that some refuges had few beds. For the first time, I carried a sleeping pad—just in case.

The no-bed-for-me-tonight fear was never realized.

But that sleeping pad became a delightful luxury. I sat on it every day while eating a picnic lunch, and sometimes unrolled it during the hottest part of the day to take a little siesta. I kept the pad strapped to the top of my backpack for quick and easy access.

Still, I consider the sleeping pad an option, not a necessity. I'd eliminate the sleeping pad if my backpack's total weight needed to be reduced.

Pillows

Don't carry one. Your sleeping bag's stuff sack filled with extra clothes makes a satisfying little pillow.

An Inexpensive, Lightweight Sleeping Pad

If you choose to take a sleeping pad, consider a closed-cell blue foam pad. It weighs and costs far less than other sleeping pads. (Some closed-cell pads come in other colors, such as gray, but these often weigh more than the blue ones.) "Closed cell" means that it doesn't need air—the material's density provides the padding.

Most sleeping pads weigh well over a half kilogram (about one pound). After I cut my blue foam pad to fit my body, it weighed 130 grams (4.6 ounces).

A pad that reaches from the shoulders to the knees is long enough. If you need to sleep on a refuge floor, use a stuff sack filled with extra clothes for a pillow. Use your emptied backpack to cover the floor below the knees.

Use Velcro straps to hold together the rolled-up pad; they weigh less than straps with metal buckles.

A disadvantage of the blue foam pad: it's not likely to last beyond one Camino journey, even if you don't use it very much. That's because it easily compresses and loses its thickness.

Heavier and thicker sleeping pads often require someone (you) to blow air into them to inflate them. These pads are thick, long, wide, made of durable fabrics, and more comfortable than a blue foam pad—and they weigh too much. They're best used for wilderness camping, where there's no chance of finding a bed at night.

Accidental Smart Shopping

I searched for "blue foam pad" on the website of a store where I'd recently bought such a pad.

There were zero matches for the search.

Over 200 "similar" items were listed, however.

They all appeared to be the expensive (heavy) sleeping pads.

Puzzled, I clicked on the very last page of the similar items.

Voilà!

The blue foam pad.

Listed as "Blue Foam Pad."

Inexpensive option, listed last.

A FRIEND'S BLUE FOAM PAD.

Staying well fed and hydrated on the Camino is just as important as making sure you have a good setup to get some rest at night. We'll take a closer look at food and water in the next chapter.

CHAPTER 7

FOOD AND WATER
Advice about the Heaviest Stuff You'll Carry

Food and water add more weight to the backpack than any other category of items. That weight diminishes during the day's walk, thank goodness, as you eat lunch and snacks and drink the water. There are times, however, when one should plan to carry extra water and food.

Using Your Guidebook for Food and Water Planning

Read ahead in your guidebook to see what resources lie ahead. Look for places where you can get water containers refilled. Notice the locations and hours of restaurants, bar-cafés, grocers, butchers, bakeries, and outdoor village markets. If you see a village or hamlet on the map, don't assume there will be access to potable water or a place to buy food.

Plan at least a day in advance. Pay particular attention to Saturday afternoons, Sundays, and even Mondays, as town and village shops, restaurants, and some bar-cafés are often closed on these days. That's when you'll need to have extra food and water.

Caution: Easter and Other Holiday Weekends

One day in France I had to ration out a bar of chocolate—my only remaining food—for breakfast, lunch, and dinner. It was Monday of the long Easter weekend—a tricky time to get food in both France and Spain. All the restaurants, bar-cafés, and shops were closed for the day in the area where I was walking. I had already eaten the "emergency" food in my backpack.

If you want to avoid every kid's dream and most adults' nightmare—chocolate for every meal—carry extra food, particularly around the long Easter weekend. This is a big holiday in both France and Spain, and although timing varies by region, it's best to plan for limited food access from the Thursday before Easter through the Monday after.

For other national holidays, ask the locals about anticipated shop or restaurant closures. It could depend on the location, with cities or large towns usually having more places that stay open.

Guessing and Padding

When organizing your backpack, guess the amount of food and water you'll need for a day's walk. Add that weight to your total backpack weight.

Then pad it a little.

Needing an extra bottle of water is a good example of why you should pad the weight estimate for food and water. You could indeed find you'll need extra water once you're on the Camino, depending on water access and the weather (particularly when it's hot).

Guessing what you'll need and padding that a little provides a more accurate, even if approximate, total backpack weight. Not adding a guesstimate for food and water creates only the illusion of a lightweight backpack.

How Much Does That Snack Weigh?

- One medium-size piece of fruit—like an apple, orange, or banana—*averages* about 200 grams (7 ounces).
- One liter of water weighs about a kilogram (2.2 pounds).

That's about 1.2 kilograms (2.6 pounds) for a piece of fruit and a bottle of water. Most pilgrims need more than that for a typical hiking day on the Camino.

Finding a Balance

If you carry more food and water than you need, efforts to trim grams for a lightweight backpack will be for naught. Think of Vidal's maxim about carrying one's fears when gathering food and water supplies on the Camino. But don't skimp, either: proper nutrition, hydration, and appropriate calorie consumption are essential for a healthy Camino journey.

Within a day or two on the Camino you'll begin to feel more confident when planning ahead for both food and water and will have a sense of the right amount to carry and the consequences of carrying too much—or too little.

Eating on the Camino

For dinner you can often find a "pilgrim's menu" at restaurants, bar-cafés, and even at some pilgrims' accommodations along the popular Camino routes. This relatively inexpensive meal typically offers three hearty courses plus wine and helps to replenish the calories you've burned during a long day's hike. It also provides one hot and nutritious meal each day.

Kitchen Facilities

There's no need to take plates, bowls, or cups on the Camino. Where there's a kitchen facility at a refuge, there's usually some crockery and cutlery. Most kitchens also have pots and pans, although sometimes a refuge has only a microwave oven—or a hotplate. Occasionally you'll find basic staples like rice or pasta left by other pilgrims. Spices, salt and pepper, and cooking oil are sometimes found too. Most pilgrims check out the facilities at their accommodations and then go to the local grocers to get what's needed for their evening meal and for breakfast the next morning.

A picnic lunch while hiking might include foods that are high in calories with relatively limited weight, like snack bars, nuts, olives, bread, a hunk of cheese, an avocado, slices of meat, or hard-boiled eggs. You can also buy small canned foods like tuna salads or squid-in-ink (the latter found in Spain). You can even carry yogurt for lunch or a snack if it's kept inside, and on top of, your backpack (so it doesn't get squashed).

A TYPICAL LUNCH ON THE VÍA DE LA PLATA ROUTE: OLIVES, WATER, AND A CHEESE *BOCADILLO* (SPANISH FOR SANDWICH).

Most pilgrims prefer to eat a light lunch, then consume snacks throughout the day to keep their energy levels high. Occasionally you'll get lucky and find yourself in a village or town around lunchtime so you can enjoy a hot meal. Caution: too much beer or wine, along with a large lunch, can make walking the final kilometers of the day extremely difficult!

You can choose between a few options for breakfast on the Camino: make your own breakfast at the pilgrims' refuge; carry breakfast foods in your backpack (like a piece of fruit, bread, and cheese); or eat breakfast at a bar-café, where you'll usually get a glass of orange juice along with the usual bread (sometimes toasted), butter, jam, and coffee.

Breakfast
Spanish = *desayuno*
French = *petit déjeuner*

Investigate the breakfast options after arriving in your destination for the day. If a bar-café or restaurant doesn't open until after you want to leave the next morning, buy breakfast foods at a local bakery or a grocery store that evening. That way you won't be hanging around for an hour or two in the morning, waiting for breakfast (some places to eat don't open their doors until after eight—and sometimes even later—in the morning).

More About Water

Water is surprisingly heavy. Bottled water is usually measured by the metric system, and one liter—a little more than a quart—weighs 1 kilogram (about 2.2 pounds).

Drinking enough water is so important while backpacking that it's better to err on the side of carrying too much. If it's clear toward the end of the walking day that you've overestimated, pour out some of the excess water on the ground—or over your head if it's hot—instead of carrying it the last few kilometers. You can then replenish your water supply after arriving at your accommodations for the night. That's a better scenario than underestimating how much water you'll need and running out. (While tap water is safe in both France and Spain, it's best to ask the locals whether the outdoor fountains provide safe drinking water.)

The amount of water to carry depends on the distance walked during a particular day, the weather, your body's needs, and resources available along the way. Again, a guidebook usually tells where water is available—and where it is not—so you can plan accordingly (we'll look at options for carrying water—water bottles and backpack hydration systems—in Chapter 12: Backpack Features to Consider).

I recently walked in the excessive heat of southern Spain. I started each day with at least two liters of water, but sometimes more when the guidebook indicated that no water was available along that day's route. When a guidebook warns about a lack of water for a long stretch of the Camino, it's a good idea to carry more than what you usually require for the same distance. Once you're familiar with the average amount of water you drink each day for a particular distance, you'll know how much extra water to take when your guidebook tells you that water is scarce.

Remember that cold-weather walking also requires a healthy supply of water. You'll still perspire in the cold, and your eyes will water and your nose will run. Moisture released from the body needs to be replaced.

Using a Bag to Organize Food-Related Items

Designate a plastic bag or a stuff sack, ideally with a drawstring, to carry all food-related items. Then when preparing a picnic lunch, for example, you can pull out the bag and have everything you need. Keep the food bag in the top of your backpack for easy access.

I use an old sleeping bag's stuff sack for a food bag. The sack has a drawstring and is laminated on the inside. That prevents liquids and gooey or sticky foods from infiltrating the contents of my backpack.

Here are some other things that should be carried in the food bag besides food:

Small Spoon

Although it's not essential, a small spoon is useful. The size that comes with a cup of tea or coffee in a restaurant works well enough for things like eating yogurt or canned tuna salad or for scooping out an avocado.

Pocketknife

Although a one-blade pocketknife is sufficient, a second blade can be useful if it's also designed to be a can opener. But toothpicks, screwdrivers, and various blade sizes add too much weight. You'll use the knife primarily for slicing picnic foods like cheese, tomatoes, or fruit.

If you're flying into Europe and won't be checking any luggage, remember that security restrictions will prevent you from bringing a knife on the plane. You can easily buy an inexpensive knife in France or Spain.

Pocketknife
Spanish = *navaja*
French = *couteau*

Bandana

This is the most versatile item you can carry in your food bag. It can be used as a picnic tablecloth, a napkin, and a washcloth. After dowsing it with water, it can be used to clean a knife blade or spoon.

If my weight budget allows, I'll take two bandanas: one for the food bag, and one I can use as a washrag or to cover my face when it's cold.

Emergency Food

A guidebook usually warns you about areas with a lack of opportunities to get food and water—but not always. I've already mentioned the long Easter weekend and other holidays that can play a factor. In addition, sometimes things change between the time a guidebook is written and the time you're walking the Camino. Restaurants, shops, or bar-cafés can suddenly close forever.

When there's no place to get food, it's necessary to improvise. For that reason, I recommend carrying emergency food in your backpack—just enough to get you through the night and into the next day.

I carry a minimal amount: a couple of tea bags, a snack bar, a packet of instant soup, and sometimes a chocolate bar or a small bag of nuts. I can usually supplement this meager fare with leftovers from lunch or snacks, like bread, cheese, almonds, olives, or dried fruit.

I've only tapped into my emergency rations a couple of times, but they saved the day. One can get mighty hungry on the Camino, especially after walking several hours in the cold, wind, and rain.

EMERGENCY FOOD BOUGHT AHEAD OF TIME—JUST IN CASE THERE WASN'T AN OPTION TO EAT
DINNER ON A SUNDAY NIGHT IN A SMALL TOWN (THERE WASN'T)

Pilgrims have no choice but to carry food and water, regardless of how much weight they add. But some other types of items truly are optional, such as technology devices.

CHAPTER 8

TECHNOLOGY
Advice about Mobile Phones and Other Devices on the Camino

Technology devices are not essential for a Camino journey. Throughout the ages, people have walked to Santiago without a mobile phone, camera, computer, GPS, digital language translator, or any other device. And many pilgrims do the same today.

On my first two Camino journeys, I carried no technology devices—not even a camera or a mobile phone. That was freedom: nothing to fuss with, nothing to charge, no reason to worry about theft when separated from my backpack. Who would want my clothes and toiletries? (Take my dirty socks, please.)

On my third Camino journey, I bought the least expensive mobile phone I could find in France. It was useful, so I took it on subsequent journeys, even though the battery charger was a weight hog in my backpack.

By my fourth Camino journey pocket-size digital cameras (no film!) had come on the market, so I started taking a camera when walking the Camino. Technological advances were beginning to seduce me . . .

So perhaps it was inevitable that I'd fall in love with the first generation of the iPhone. This device is much more than a mobile phone; it's also an address book, flashlight, calculator, alarm clock, calendar, language dictionary, and a camera (iPhones now have video cameras too, although I still use a pocket-size camera because it has more settings and better storage for photographs and video). The iPhone holds a dozen books and various documents. It surfs the web and sends and receives email. All in one compact device. Even the battery charger is so slight that I don't worry about its weight inside my backpack.

Of course the iPhone isn't the only smartphone available. Phones that use the Android software and Blackberry smartphones offer similar features and functions.

To decide which approach is right for you, ask yourself: Will tech devices enhance my journey and/or save weight? Or will they become a burden?

After all, if millions of people over the past thousand years have walked the Camino without this stuff, so can we.

General Information

The following sections provide only general information about the tech devices most commonly used on the Camino. We'll also look at a few devices that novice pilgrims might be tempted to take. For those who've never been on the Camino, it's understandably difficult to know what to expect on the journey.

The purpose of this information is to help you decide what to take—or what not to take. But because choices are numerous, and technology is changing rapidly, I won't recommend any particular devices.

For the latest information, go to the Camino forums (www.caminodesantiago.me and www.caminodesantiago.me.uk) to ask questions and read what others are saying about technology on the Camino.

Camera

Digital cameras are perfect for backpackers: no film canisters, lightweight battery chargers, and the ability to store thousands of pictures on tiny memory cards. You can quickly grab a small camera from a pocket to catch moving critters before they vanish.

SCENE FROM THE MIDDLE AGES TODAY (PHOTO TAKEN WITH A POCKET-SIZE DIGITAL CAMERA),
VÉZELAY ROUTE, FRANCE

Mobile Phone

A mobile phone isn't essential on the Camino, but it's helpful. Here are some country-specific considerations.

France

Sometimes the only place to stay on the French routes is an inn, a private refuge, or a Pilgrim-sympathetic home, and reservations might be encouraged—or even required. Consult your guidebook at least a day or two in advance for reservation information.

It's easier to make reservations if you have your own phone, but it's certainly possible to walk the Le Puy or Vézelay routes without a mobile phone. If you can't find a functioning pay phone, you can often make a metered phone call at a bar-café or a hotel. (A metered phone keeps track of the length of the call; you then pay the business owner directly.)

Also, the proprietor of a private accommodation might graciously help by calling ahead to make your reservation for the next night.

Spain

Most of the pilgrim-specific accommodations on the routes in Spain do not take reservations.

When walking during the popular Camino seasons, and on weekends or holidays, call ahead to make reservations at private accommodations such as hotels or inns.

As in France, if you can't find a working pay phone, ask at a bar-café or hotel if there's a metered phone you can use.

Prepaid Phone Cards

You can buy prepaid cards for pay phones at news agents, tobacco shops, and many grocery stores in France and Spain. It's rare for a pay phone to take coins these days, so a phone card is essential if you're planning to use pay phones.

Taking Your Own Mobile Phone to Europe

Review your owner's manual, or call your service provider, to find out if your mobile phone has the correct specifications to work in France or Spain. If not, see the following sections Buying a Mobile Phone in Europe and Buying a Travel Phone Before Leaving Home for other options.

If your phone will work abroad, there are two possibilities for using it on the Camino: pay your service provider's fees for international roaming, or buy a SIM card in Europe.

Pay Your Service Provider's Fees for International Roaming

If you want to use your phone but it is "locked"—that is, limited to work only on your service provider's network—your only choice is to pay your service provider's roaming fees. Arrange for the best international plan and be sure to ask if your phone's international roaming potential is "active" (so you can be sure it will actually work once you're in Europe).

Some pilgrims may want to unlock, or "jailbreak," their phone to be able to use it on European phone networks, which would no doubt be less costly. You can find information for how to do this online—but also read up on the risks involved. Independent phone shops might also offer to unlock your phone.

If your phone is not locked, then you have another option, possibly the least costly way to make phone calls in Europe from your own mobile phone: buying a SIM card.

Buy a SIM (Subscriber Identity Module) Card from a European Mobile-Phone Shop

The SIM card is a small data-holding chip that is inserted into your phone. Buying a SIM card in Europe gives you a local phone number.

For example: if you buy a SIM card in France and insert it into your phone, you'll have a French phone number and the ability to access the French cellular networks at local rates.

The French SIM card (and thus the phone) may not work once you cross the border into Spain, however, and if it does, the roaming charges could be expensive. The best option is to buy another SIM card after arriving in Spain. Then you'll have a Spanish phone number and access to the Spanish cellular networks at local rates.

Sometimes you can buy a SIM card at an airport store or kiosk after you arrive at your destination. Or ask at the front desk of your accommodations the first night where the nearest mobile-phone shop is located.

Buying a Mobile Phone in Europe

Buying a mobile phone in Europe is usually a better deal than renting a phone before you leave. The price range is about €50-100 (that should include some minutes to get you started). Any city or town in France and Spain has plenty of stores that sell mobile phones.

It's relatively easy to buy a phone in Europe—just be sure to bring your passport with you to the shop: identification is required when buying a mobile phone. If you're not very fluent in French or Spanish, getting what you want could be a challenge. (Buying a phone is more complicated than buying tapas or a croissant.) You may get lucky and find someone behind the counter who speaks English, or an English-speaking customer might be willing to help you out. But it's best to take a dictionary or phrase book in case you need it.

Spanish

Pay as you go (phone plan) = *de pre pago* or *prepagado*
SIM card = *tarjeta SIM*
Unlock my phone = *desbloquear mi teléfono*
Unlocked phone = *teléfono libre*

French

Pay as you go (phone plan) = *payable à la communication* or *forfait à carte*

SIM card = *carte SIM*
Unlock my phone = *déverrouiller mon telephone*
Unlocked phone = *telephone déverrouillé*

(For more specific language help, visit www.wordreference. com for a free translation dictionary. The site also has forums where you can ask specific language-usage questions.)

If you're crossing the French-Spanish border on your pilgrimage, make sure the phone is unlocked. Then you can change the SIM card after crossing the border, allowing you to pay local rates instead of out-of-country roaming charges.

Get a "pay ahead" (pay as you go) phone plan. Then it's easy to buy more time for the phone at grocery stores, smoke shops, or news agents. After paying a cashier in a shop you'll receive a receipt with a set of numbers; enter these numbers into the phone to activate the credit.

Buying a Travel Phone Before Leaving Home

For those who prefer to avoid any language challenges they might encounter in a French or Spanish mobile-phone store, here are three companies that offer international phones for sale or for rent, and where you can also purchase international SIM cards (I have not used them, so I cannot personally recommend one over the other):

- www.cellularabroad.com
- www.planetomni.com
- www.telestial.com

A Caution for Smartphones

As I mentioned earlier, a smartphone can save weight by serving multiple functions, thus eliminating the need to bring other items.

One note of caution, however. Most data plans for smartphones and other mobile phones with data downloading capabilities charge by the kilobyte, and these charges can add up fast. One email with a photo attached may cost you more to download than you'll pay for a night at a pilgrims' accommodation.

Other apps, especially those that identify your location as a part of their function—such as GPS (Global Positioning System) applications—can also be quite expensive to use when abroad.

Check with your service provider before leaving home. Setting up an international data roaming plan might prevent outrageous phone bills. And it's a good idea to also confirm whether sending an SMS—a text message—is always less expensive than making a phone call.

Otherwise, shut off incoming email and other data-rich functions when you're not in a free Wi-Fi area.

A Caution for All Mobile Phones

Petty thieves love mobile phones because they're easy to grab out of your hand. Be especially careful when using your mobile phone in the subway, on a bus, or when riding a suburban train. A thief can quickly snatch the phone then jump out at the next stop. In late 2010 the Paris police chief said that nearly half of the thefts on public transportation systems involved a mobile phone—more than wallets or purses. It's likely that this type of theft is not unique to Paris, so it's wise to use caution in other cities as well.

VoIP Calls

It's also worth investigating internet-based voice services, also known as VoIP (Voice over Internet Protocol) calls. They're increasingly seen as one of the most inexpensive ways for international travelers to make phone calls using wireless, 3G, or 4G data access from mobile devices. Some even offer free international calls. But here's a caution and a caveat:

- Caution: Be careful when using a 3G or 4G connection for VoIP calls abroad, or you may find yourself racking up expensive data roaming fees from your phone's regular service provider. Consider using a wireless connection instead.
- Caveat: Some VoIP providers provide free or inexpensive calls only if both parties are using the application provided by the VoIP provider. It's a good idea to investigate the details before leaving home so you know what to expect.

Here are three examples of VoIP providers as of this writing. Skype can be used from a computer with an internet connection, but so far Viber and Truphone only provide apps for mobile devices, including some tablet computers. To keep up with the latest information on this rapidly developing technology, Google "VoIP calls" to find more options.

- Skype: www.skype.com
- Truphone: www.truphone.com
- Viber: www.viber.com

Wi-Fi on the Camino

You can find free wireless internet (Wi-Fi) hotspots along the Camino routes. If you're carrying a smartphone or other device with Wi-Fi, these hotspots offer the best opportunity to check email, use map applications, browse the internet, or use other data-rich functions.

The most recent editions of guidebooks will mention where Wi-Fi is available. Hotels, cafés, libraries, and municipal buildings are good places to look for Wi-Fi when your guidebook lacks information for a particular locale.

Laptops, Netbooks, iPads, and Other Tablets

If you feel that one of these devices will enhance your journey, and won't be a burden, why not bring it? Just be sure to consider the added weight versus the benefits and amount of use. Also consider that guidebooks usually tell you where you can find a computer with internet access along the Camino. Many pilgrims use these access points to upload photos and to communicate with friends and loved ones back home.

Generally, I wouldn't recommend taking any of these devices. One of the most beloved of all aspects of the Camino experience is the camaraderie with other pilgrims. A computer could turn out to be a barrier.

I understand, however, that each person has his or her own particular needs and uses for these devices; make the decision that is best for you.

Digital Music Player

Some music players and their earbuds are so tiny and lightweight that they're irresistible. Sometimes it's a pleasure to listen to music before going to sleep at night. In a crowded pilgrims' refuge, a digital music player can create a little psychological space. If you suspect you might need to balance camaraderie with a bit of privacy, a digital music player is a great resource.

I've never seen a pilgrim listen to music while walking, although it's likely some have. I'd guess that most pilgrims feel that the birds and breezes make the best music. Silence is popular on the Camino.

Pilgrim Stories

I had no idea real cuckoo birds existed—I thought they were only in Swiss clocks—until I walked the Camino and heard their unique call in the nearby woods. I confessed this to a Swiss pilgrim, and she told me that the Swiss also made the cuckoos in the woods.

If your digital music device can also serve as an address book or a language dictionary, and perhaps many other functions, it's worth its weight as a multipurpose device.

The light emitted from a digital music player's or mobile phone's screen allows it to function as a flashlight too; it's at least enough light to show the next few steps in front of you on the way to a toilet in the middle of the night.

Digital Language Translator

No device yet exists where you can speak any phrase into it and receive back the exact translation (despite advertising that says a device can do just that). There are just too many ways to say something. A common phrase in one language is not said the same way in another. Even English has variations: a "torch" is a "flashlight." "Take away" food is food "to go."

Copy and paste a chunk of text from any foreign-language website into an online translator to convert the foreign phrase into

English. In the resulting translation you're likely to see examples of what you might consider an odd way of saying things. The translation might even be incomprehensible.

Nevertheless, translation devices are sometimes helpful. The most useful among them provide features to learn the language, and of course a translation dictionary.

If your weight budget allows for a translator, and using it will encourage you to communicate more, take it. Or consider a pocket-size language dictionary or phrase book—there are no batteries to charge, and it's probably less costly.

GPS

A GPS (global positioning system) provides navigational assistance via signals received from orbiting satellites. In cities, these devices tell you the driving route and the distance from one point to another.

On the Camino, GPS information is not as precise (at least not yet). If you get a good signal, the GPS device might tell you the distance from where you're standing to the next town or village.

But a GPS device won't show any details—the twists and turns—of a Camino trail.

Until a specific and reliable application is designed for the Camino routes (apparently some are working on it—check the store that sells apps for your device), it's more accurate to follow the ubiquitous Camino signs and symbols.

Besides, a pilgrim already has enough information to approximate where he or she is at any given time. Most pilgrims walk about four kilometers per hour. Considering the time already walked, and the distance between reference points provided in the guidebook, you can get a good estimate of where you are and how much farther you have to walk.

Avoid "Frying" Tech Devices
Voltage Converters and Adapter Plugs

French and Spanish electrical outlets use 220 volts; make sure your device is capable of using that voltage. Most newer devices indicate the voltage on the plug or AC adapter or on the device itself, and some can handle a range of voltages (look for something like "input 100–240V").

If your device can only handle a lower voltage, you'll need a voltage converter to avoid damaging the device with too much electrical current.

Caution: If you're taking a computer, be especially careful. Many new computers and other electronics are equipped for 100–240 volts, but if yours is not and you need to use a converter, note that some voltage converters say, "Do not use with a computer." Be sure the converter you get has the capacity to work specifically with computers—or you'll risk damaging your computer.

Electrical outlets in France and Spain use prongs that might be different from the ones in your home country (search Google Images for "Spanish electrical outlets" or "French electrical outlets" to see them).

If your device has a different type of plug, you'll need an adapter plug so you can plug your device into the electric socket. Grounded adapter plugs provide protection against power surges. **Adapter plugs *do not* convert voltage;** they only allow the plug to fit into a foreign electrical outlet.

Some devices may need both a converter and an adapter.
Other devices are dual voltage, and may need only the adapter plug.

Amazon.com is a good place to see an array of voltage converters and adapters as well as photos. Travel agents and travel stores are also a great source of information on this topic.

———————

Which technology items to take on the Camino is a very personal choice, as is choosing toiletries and first aid items. We'll look at these in the next chapter.

CHAPTER 9

TOILETRIES AND FIRST AID
Tips for What to Take

I met a delightful French woman in her late fifties on the Le Puy route in France. It was her first pilgrimage. She had been walking for only three days and was already feeling a serious pain in one of her legs. Her son, a doctor, had advised by phone that she should eliminate weight from her backpack.

The French woman asked a Canadian woman she had recently befriended to help her reorganize her backpack. I was sitting on a bunk nearby when I heard the Canadian woman ask her to spread out the contents of her backpack. Soon I saw a pile of stuff smothering two twin beds in the pilgrims' refuge. I looked up again when I heard the Canadian woman declaring, "These must go!" She was pointing at four full rolls of toilet paper. The French woman agreed to let go of her scarcity fears and banished the rolls to the refuge's bathroom. Later, when I joined the two of them for dinner, the French woman stated that she was determined to make it to Santiago de Compostela—no matter what.

Several weeks later, I heard that she (and her lighter backpack) had made it to Santiago. She'd walked about 1,600 kilometers (1,000 miles).

No matter what Camino route you take, know that you can easily replenish toiletry items on the Camino. Even small village shops carry the basics: shampoo, soap, toothpaste—and toilet paper.

Toiletries: Think Small

Take lightweight sample-size toiletry products. The idea is to eliminate weight and bulk.

I've found most of my sample-size products and small plastic containers at a chain grocery store. Apparently the market for sample sizes—especially of liquids and lotions—has increased along with air transportation security restrictions. Outdoor stores that sell backpacking gear also sell sample-size toiletry products and empty containers. If you can't find the items you want in a sample size, buy small plastic containers and fill them with your preferred products. If you need to replenish something along the way, but can't find a sample size, see if you can share the larger quantity with another pilgrim. Or, take what you need and ask the pilgrims' refuge if you can leave the larger bottle or package behind for other pilgrims to replenish their own supplies.

Bringing only small amounts of toiletry items saves weight that might be better used on something else. An average-size tube of toothpaste weighs 226 grams (8 ounces). My sample-size toothpaste tube weighs 29 grams (1 ounce). Weight savings: about 198 grams (7 ounces).

That savings equals the weight of my down vest.

Toiletries: A List for the Minimalist

Store the following in a ziplock bag; it's the lightest-weight carrying option.

- **Toothpaste:** a sample-size tube weighs much less than a regular-size tube.
- **Toothbrush:** travel-size toothbrushes often have a cap that can be used to extend the length of the handle.
- **Dental floss:** a sample size might last your entire Camino journey.
- **Comb or brush:** take the smallest one you can find.
- **Shampoo:** get a sample size, fill a small plastic bottle, or use a multipurpose bar or liquid that also works as a body soap—and even as laundry soap for washing socks and underwear.

- **Bar or liquid soap**: keep a bar of soap in a *flimsy* sandwich baggie. This somehow allows the bar to dry between uses. Sturdier or slicker plastic bags cause the bar to stay wet, so it eventually turns gooey. Hard-plastic bar-soap holders often create the same gooey problem (and they weigh more).
- **Deodorant:** bar or liquid; choose the lightest in weight.
- **Toenail clippers:** trimmed toenails keep feet happy on the Camino.
- **Pack towel:** a backpacker or travel towel weighs less, is less bulky, and dries faster than a typical bath towel.
- **Toilet paper:** take a partial roll and squish it so you can take out the paper tube for less weight and bulk. Or, buy a travel size, which comes in a tight roll of about fifty sheets. TIP: When you use a public facility on the Camino, stuff your pocket with a little TP to use along the trail—or at the next public facility where you're faced with an empty roll. This is an international dilemma for women, though diplomats never talk about it.
- **Tissues:** just one small packet. Can also double as TP. Replenish along the way.
- **Tampons or pads:** can be bought along the Camino. Take enough for two periods at the most.

Shaving Beards, Underarms, and Legs on the Camino

Sometimes there's not much privacy, or hot water, in pilgrims' refuges. There's often a line to use shower or sink facilities.

To simplify your *toilette,* consider going wild on your Camino journey. This way you'll also save weight on razor blades, razors, and shaving foam or soap.

Men: if you've never seen yourself in a beard, or it's been a long time, this is the chance to check it out.

Women: if you've shaved your legs since you were a teenager, you might be surprised to discover how pleasurable a warm breeze feels on hairy legs. Also consider going au naturel under the arms while you're walking the Camino. Besides, imagine this: men shaving their legs and underarms. Sounds strange, doesn't it? Why do women go to that trouble, but men don't? The Camino pilgrimage offers women a chance to try something different too.

First Aid
Backpacker's First Aid Kit

A prepackaged backpacker's first aid kit typically comes with sterile dressings, different sizes and types of adhesive bandages, tape, ibuprofen, antihistamines, antibiotic ointment, treated wipes for cleaning cuts, moleskin pieces for blisters, and sometimes a couple of safety pins. Everything is contained in a compact waterproof packet. The size I take fits in the palm of my hand.

The number of items contained in the kit determines its size and weight. The heaviest backpacker's first aid kit I've seen weighed about a kilogram (more than two pounds)—a mini-hospital, or a hypochondriac's dream kit.

I prefer the ultralight version for the Camino, because it only weighs 99 grams (about 3.5 ounces). One can always supplement the kit by buying items at the local pharmacies frequently found along Camino routes.

Personal Medications

Check with your doctor regarding any medications you'll need while you're on the Camino. Be sure to take enough for the entire time you'll be gone, as well as copies of prescriptions, should you need refills.

Small Scissors

To cut bandages and gauze and for other miscellaneous tasks, take a tiny pair of scissors. I buy a small size that fits into my backpacker's first aid kit.

If you're flying to Europe and won't be checking any luggage, it's likely that security won't let you take scissors on the plane. You can easily buy a small pair of scissors upon arrival in France or Spain.

Scissors
Spanish = *tijeras*
French = *ciseaux*

Blister Treatment

I once checked out a book from the library that was devoted entirely to the care of the feet. In the chapter on blisters, over a hundred backpackers, runners, and other athletes offered their advice for the prevention and treatment of blisters. All types of adhesive tapes, powders, creams, ointments, "skins," and socks were suggested.

I soon realized that one contributor's advice often contradicted another's. One backpacker swore that duct tape prevented blisters; another emphatically disagreed and wrote that duct tape *causes* blisters. He then offered his own solution, which was then contradicted by another contributor's method for blister prevention.

Apparently, the author enlisted such advice because he knew he couldn't provide a definitive answer on the one true way to prevent and treat blisters. And neither can I.

Blisters are by far the most common ailment on the Camino, and everyone has their own methods for prevention and treatment. Even pharmacies along the popular Camino routes sometimes specialize in blister-treatment products and advice.

Because I haven't found the perfect solution to prevent or treat blisters, I can only provide a list of what I find most useful.

Toe Gel Caps

Toe gel caps slip over the toes. Made of an oil-impregnated silicone gel, they're lightweight, soft, and flexible. Packages of toe gel caps usually come in four sizes so you can get a close-enough fit for your baby toes, big toes, and those in between—then easily cut them for an even better fit.

At the first hint of a blister forming on a toe, I slip a toe gel cap on that toe to stop the problem. The caps are also great for covering calluses on the bottom or side of a toe.

Toe gel caps are sometimes difficult to find; I buy mine from Feet Relief (www.feetrelief.com). They're based in San Francisco but sell internationally. They also have a variety of other products to prevent or relieve problems with the feet (click on "Products" at the top of their website to navigate your way to the toe caps).

Gentle Paper Tape

This extremely thin tape is often used by athletes to cover areas that might experience friction. It's great for hot spots where that first hint of heat indicates a blister getting ready to be born. But if a blister has already formed, the gentle paper tape will probably be too thin to help.

Compeed

Compeed is a brand name for a kind of thick adhesive bandage that can be used to cover a blister. They're available in almost every pharmacy in France and Spain, both on and off the Camino routes. Various sizes and shapes are available to protect heels, soles, and toes of all sizes. Compeed bandages have some distinct advantages and disadvantages.

Compeed advantages:

- Once applied, they stay on—even when showering.
- The thickness of the bandage helps to cushion the blister, so it won't get worse from more friction or pressure. It also helps to eliminate some of the pain caused by the blister.
- Application is easy and quick.

Compeed disadvantages:

- They get gooey and sticky when wet from foot perspiration.
- They'll also get wet from a shower. Let them dry thoroughly before putting on socks.
- That gooey stickiness can stick to the inside of socks and is almost impossible to scrape or wash off.

PILGRIMS SOMETIMES GRAB SHEEP'S WOOL STUCK ON FENCES, THEN PUT A CLUMP OF THAT WOOL IN THEIR FOOTWEAR TO HELP PREVENT BLISTERS. (YOU'LL SEE COUNTLESS SHEEP ON ALL THE CAMINO ROUTES; THIS FLUFFY FELLOW WAS ON THE VÉZELAY ROUTE IN FRANCE.)

In addition to toiletries and first aid items, there are a lot of other small, useful things you might want to consider adding to your pack.

CHAPTER 10

USEFUL SMALL ITEMS
A Detailed List

Although some pilgrims might want to use all of the following small items, they're only suggestions for what might be useful on a Camino pilgrimage. As always: take only what you'll actually use.

Earplugs!

I kept the exclamation mark from my notes, as in "Don't forget to mention earplugs!" They're an essential item, especially for light sleepers. In the shared sleeping quarters of pilgrims' accommodations, you'll hear the pilgrim night music—snoring. To be able to get some rest in communal accommodations, most pilgrims use earplugs.

You can easily find earplugs at pharmacies in France and Spain. If you don't speak French or Spanish, you can just plug your ears with your fingers and make a snoring sound. You'll get a laugh and the earplugs.

Money Belt

For over a thousand years, scoundrels have ripped off pilgrims on the Camino. Today, thieves are rare but not unheard-of.

Bulging fanny packs were once a popular way for travelers to store their valuables. Thieves loved them because they were so obvious.

It's now recognized that discretion is better, and it's a good idea to keep valuables out of sight. Most savvy travelers use a money belt, which is a slim pouch with at least one zippered compartment.

Worn around the waist, it's held in place by an elastic strap with a secure clip. The money belt is a secure place to carry your passport, credit cards, extra cash, plane tickets or e-ticket printouts, and other important information such as addresses and phone numbers. It's much roomier than the other kind of "money belt"—a leather or cloth belt that looks just like a regular belt and has a zippered interior pocket that only holds a small amount of cash.

Some wear the money belt inside their pants, while others wear it on the outside. For me, it depends: in touristy areas, bus stations, and train stations—where theft is more likely—I'll wear the money belt *inside* my pants. Most of the time, however, the money belt is more comfortably worn *outside* the pants, especially while backpacking on the Camino. That's why I like wearing a long-tailed shirt: it covers the money belt's placement on my rear, keeping it out of sight.

Money-Belt Alternatives

For those who don't like the idea of wearing a money belt around the waist, there are other options. One of these is called a "hidden pocket," or sometimes a "secret wallet." This has a slim pouch, like the money belt I've just described for travelers, and a cord that attaches the pouch to a regular hold-up-the-pants belt so the pouch can then be tucked inside the pants (usually at the hip). Another alternative is a "neck wallet" or "neck pouch." These are also similar to the traveler's money belt, but an attached cord allows you to hang it around your neck so it lies against your chest. Less used, another option is the undercover leg pouch (sometimes called an undercover leg stash). It also has features similar to the traveler's money belt, but straps secure the pouch to your leg.

Coin Purse or Wallet

As a partner for the money belt, consider using a coin purse or wallet for the small amounts of money you'll use every day; keep it in a pocket for quick and easy access. Then you won't have to expose your money belt for every minor transaction. You can also quickly put cash there after visiting an ATM and thus avoid exposing your money belt in public.

Security Tips While Staying at a Pilgrims' Refuge
Precaution = Security

- Sleep with your money belt at the bottom of your sleeping bag, by your feet.
- Keep your money belt near you in a waterproof bag while showering in communal facilities.
- Don't leave valuables at the refuge when eating out or visiting local sights.
- If your smartphone, tablet computer, or other digital device holds important information like bank account numbers, passwords, or addresses that you wouldn't want others to see, lock the device with a pass code after each use.

Mini-Backpack

Consider bringing an ultralight mini-backpack to carry things while sightseeing or doing errands in late afternoon or evening. I use mine to carry a jacket, camera, cell phone, water bottle, journal, and pen. I use it to carry food bought at groceries and bakeries. I also use it to carry food and water on flights to and from Europe.

Mini-backpacks stuff into their own outside pocket. Post-stuffing, the pack fits into the palm of the hand. Made of a thin nylon fabric, it has no features: just the body of the pack, two thin shoulder straps, and the tiny outside pocket it stuffs into.

To save a couple of grams, I cut off the thick plastic zipper grip and an unneeded metal hook.

Small Calculator

A calculator can be used for calculating kilometers (all distances are measured in kilometers on the Camino) and other planning. It can also be helpful for currency conversions. Find a credit card–size calculator that will easily tuck into a money belt. You won't need to carry a separate calculator if you take a mobile phone with a calculator function.

Address Book

The lightest option: write the addresses you need on one piece of paper, using both sides if needed. Then keep it safe in your money belt—it's difficult to replace when you're a long way from home.

Add other important information to the list, such as phone numbers to report lost credit cards, airline contact information, flight confirmation numbers, and email addresses.

Or, use your mobile phone to store addresses and other information. If your guidebook indicates you'll have regular internet access, you can also send an email to yourself with important information, and then access that via your online email provider. This method is also a good back-up plan regardless of how you carry addresses and other important information.

Calendar

On the Camino, time is measured by the sun's rise and fall. But sometimes it's helpful to glance at a calendar so you don't forget to go home. A calendar also helps when you need to adjust Camino walking plans.

Many mobile phones have calendars. If that's not an option, you can download a calendar from the web, or print the month(s) you need from your computer's calendar application.

I use a more old-fashioned method. First, I cut out the tiny preview months from a traditional wall calendar. I then tape those to the inside cover of a memo pad, which serves as my journal.

Journal and Pen

A lightweight journal recommendation: the just-mentioned memo pad, which fits into a shirt pocket. A fine-point pen helps you write small.

A journal stores the day's thoughts, feelings, impressions, and stories. A memo pad in the pocket can also be pulled out quickly to note newly discovered French or Spanish words, addresses of new pilgrim friends, or a local's map showing a shortcut back to the Camino route.

Those notes, words, addresses, and maps add a charm and immediacy to the journal, making it a nice memento of your journey.

Flashlight

I've carried a small flashlight on the Camino a few times, but never once used it. Usually there is enough light in accommodations to find the toilet at night, which is the most common use for a flashlight.

While I consider the flashlight an optional item, others might feel more comfortable taking one. If you decide to take a flashlight, find a tiny one, like the kind attached to a keychain. I found one that weighs only 13 grams (0.5 ounce). Or, if you take a digital music player or a mobile phone, just use that: the screen will emit enough light to see a few steps in front of you in the dark or help you search through your backpack after lights out. Or look for a flashlight app for your mobile phone. Some of these have the same projection power as the tiny flashlights.

Language Dictionary

Use a *pocket-size* French or Spanish dictionary or phrase book. Or use a translation application that can be uploaded to your mobile phone.

If you're tempted to take a separate digital translation device, consider the weight. If translating is its only function, is it worth the weight? Don't forget that it will require a charging device or batteries too.

However, as mentioned in Chapter 8: Technology, if you feel that using a translation device will give you more courage to communicate in a foreign language, then take one! Talking with the locals greatly enhances the Camino journey.

When You Don't Speak the Local Language

A small language dictionary or phrase book works well enough—and doesn't need to be recharged, either. You'll find that a lot can be communicated with just a word or two:

- *Banque?* (French for bank)
- *Farmacia?* (Spanish for pharmacy)
- *Hotel?* (the same in English, Spanish, and French—although the French word is written as *hôtel,* it's similarly pronounced)

Tip: add an upward inflection at the end of any of these words to indicate a question, and your message will be clear.

As you can see by these examples, many French and Spanish words are similar to their English counterparts—and that makes them easy to remember once you've encountered them a time or two.

Plus, communication is much more than words. You can draw maps or simple pictures, point fingers, and use facial expressions.

Most important: keep a sense of humor. Everyone feels like a three-year-old child when trying a new language. If you accidentally call someone a turnip, they'll know that you didn't mean any offense. And you can always hit the trail again, fast, when you're embarrassed.

Whistle

A whistle can be useful to annoy and confuse aggressive dogs occasionally encountered on the Camino—the high pitch hurts their ears. Keep it in an outside pocket while walking.

I've found mixed reviews on high-tech sound devices, so I take a regular whistle, like the type that's small enough to attach to a keychain.

On the Camino
Whistle + Walking Stick = Dog's Tail Between Legs

Sunglasses

Wraparound-style sunglasses help prevent dust from getting in your eyes—and also eliminate peripheral glare. A lightweight case protects them in the backpack when they're not being worn.

Extra Eyeglasses

If you wear glasses, especially prescription eyeglasses, take an extra pair.

Print Magnifier

A magnifier is helpful for seeing tiny details on maps. A credit card–size magnifier, made of a hard plastic, is the lightest in weight. A small magnifier with a light could also double as a mini-flashlight.

Lip Balm

This is the ultimate lightweight item, but you should weigh it anyway. Remember, every gram contributes to another kilogram, and every small item counts in the total backpack weight.

Hand Sanitizer

Choose a pocket-size bottle of hand sanitizer for personal hygiene during the day's walk.

Sunscreen

Since sunscreen can easily be replenished along the Camino, start out with a sample-size bottle.

Clothespins or Safety Pins

Clothespins can be scarce at pilgrims' accommodations, or not available at inns or hotels. They're worth bringing with you to hang socks, undies, a pack towel, or other items to dry.

Safety-pin advantage: As mentioned before, two socks can be be pinned together to make an emergency ear band if it's cold. Safety pins are also handy if you find yourself with a broken zipper.

Wristwatch

Leave a beloved watch at home. Since the watch you use on the Camino is likely to get wet, especially if you wear a baggy-sleeved poncho, choose a waterproof watch.

Bandana

Bandanas are incredibly versatile.

Consider taking two bandanas. One can be used as a table cloth and napkin, and to clean a knife or spoon. Use a second bandana:

- To wet and wipe your face in extreme heat
- To cover your face, bandit-style, when it's very cold or as a defense against buzzing flies or other insects
- As a washrag
- To cover the back of the neck under an intense sun

String or Thin Cord

Like safety pins, a short length of string or cord can solve many problems. I've used a thin cord to securely attach the traditional pilgrim shell to the outside of my backpack. I've used string to tie still-wet socks to the outside of my backpack, so they can dry while I hike. The string can also be used as a mini-clothesline.

———————

Once your backpack's contents are planned out, it's important not to let all your hard work go to waste by loading yourself down with books and maps. These important items can also be trimmed down for a lightweight backpack, as you'll see in the next chapter.

CHAPTER 11

GUIDEBOOKS AND MAPS (DIGITAL AND PRINT) AND THE PILGRIM'S CREDENTIAL
What Items You'll Need and Where to Find Them

A guidebook provides details for a Camino route. It lists the distances between cities, towns, and villages and tells you when to turn right or left and when to continue straight ahead (which is helpful when trail markers are scarce or unclear). It also lets you know what the terrain is like; where to sleep and eat; and where to find an ATM, transportation, and help. A guidebook also offers information about local sights and shares stories about a place and its people. Sometimes a map is included in the guidebook, although it's usually just a rough sketch. That's when a route map can come in handy.

A route map provides a detailed visual orientation to supplement your guidebook. It shows the context of where you are in relation to other places. So, for example, you might see a village a few kilometers off the trail where there might be a bar-café. A detailed map shows where to leave the trail to get to the village—and maybe even how you could pick up the trail again without backtracking. Or a map might show a lake near the trail where you could eat lunch and have a siesta.

How to Eliminate Paper Weight

- Take only essential guidebook pages.
- Tear out extraneous information like gear lists, descriptions of flora and fauna, and historical background.
- Remove the book's front and back covers.
- Trim the page margins.
- Throw away guidebook pages and maps after using them, or mail them home. (Your guidebook's weight should diminish every day.)
- Cut maps to only cover the areas you're walking through.

As mentioned before, on my last journey **I saved 494 grams (about 1 pound, 1 ounce)** just by cutting the extra paper out of guidebooks and off maps.

A detailed route map can also help you find an alternate route when there's a problem on the trail—like a bridge destroyed by a recent storm. Or the map might help you determine the direction to go when roadwork removes all the Camino trail markers at an intersection. Sometimes Mother Nature changes the trail markers too: I once arrived at a crossroads to find an old tree had collapsed; the painted trail marker was lying on the ground on a piece of bark. Since the guidebook was not clear on which direction to head (as sometimes happens), the route map helped me to figure out which trail to take, and I soon found another trail marker confirming I was on the right path.

Packing Tips

The essential guides for the Camino routes are the guidebook and the trail markers. But a detailed route map can be a helpful supplement for your journey. If a map is available for the route you plan to take (not all routes have detailed maps available), I'd recommend taking one with you.

It's important to keep your printed map and guidebook pages dry. The lightest choice for protecting them is a clear plastic ziplock bag. A drawback to using digital guidebooks or maps is that the display device (like a mobile phone, or an iPad or other tablet computer) could get wet—it might be raining hard just at the moment when you need to pull out your digital map to know whether you should turn right or left at a crossroads. Adequate shelter is not always available, like on the open plains or in a pine forest where raindrops fall easily through the skinny branches, and a digital device might become permanently damaged if it gets wet.

There are Camino guidebooks in many languages. For English speakers, a great place to look for guidebooks is the Confraternity of Saint James in London. They publish guidebooks for all the routes and sell them in their bookshop online at www.csj.org.uk (see Resources for more guidebook-buying options).

A guidebook will tell you what maps you need, if any. One guidebook for the Vézelay route, for example, includes detailed maps along with the text describing the route in detail—so there's no need to supplement that guidebook with another route map.

Every Camino route is different, with varying degrees of organized infrastructure such as places to stay within a reasonable walking distance or general help and support for pilgrims on their way to Santiago de Compostela. Usually the most up-to-date guidebooks and maps are for the most popular Camino routes, such as the Camino Francés (by far the most popular) or the Le Puy route in France.

On the Camino

If you're walking through both France and Spain, from the location of your starting point in France you can mail yourself the Spanish guidebook (and map, if you have one) to a town or city near where you'll cross the border—such as to St. Jean Pied-de-Port in France, which is the beginning of the Camino Francés route. That might be safer than mailing it from your home outside of Europe using the Poste Restante (general delivery) method that's been used by travelers for years (unfortunately, recent security concerns have made that option a bit uncertain). The local French post office where you mail the package from can help you with the postal code and the best way to write your name and address.

Digital Guidebooks and Camino Apps

If you'd like to investigate digital guidebooks or apps that are specific to the Camino, here are a few places to start your search.

Cicerone: This U.K. publisher sells English-language Camino guidebooks in both ebook and print formats. For example, you can buy ebooks for the Le Puy route (title: *The Way of Saint James— France*), the Vía de la Plata route (title: *Vía de la Plata*), and the Camino Francés route (title: *The Way of Saint James*). Visit their website, www.cicerone.co.uk, for more information on compatible digital devices and computer applications for their ebooks.

Apple iTunes App Store: You can access Apple's App Store using your Apple device or iTunes on your computer. Search on the term "Camino" to bring up the latest apps that relate to the Camino de Santiago. You'll need an Apple device, such as an iPad, iPhone, or iPod Touch, to use the apps.

Android Market: Google's operating system called Android is used on numerous digital devices; the Android app store can be found at https://market.android.com. Again, do a "Camino" search to find out if any relevant apps are available.

Amazon's App Store: Amazon also sells apps for devices that use Google's Android operating system. Go to www.amazon.com and look for the link to their app store.

Confraternity of Saint James: The organization that exists to help Camino pilgrims also provides digital access to some Camino guides (see www.csj.org.uk).

Gear Guide

Some Camino apps require an internet connection or 3G access (or later technology, starting with 4G). These connections are often not available on the mostly rural Camino trails. And if you do find access through mobile-phone towers (3G or 4G+), the data usage on your device could be expensive, so it's a good idea to read the specifics on how a particular app works.

General Orientation Map

Consider taking a map of Spain, France, or western Europe to use for general orientation and trip planning.

For example, here's how I've used these maps:

- After arriving in Santiago de Compostela, a map of western Europe helped me plan a trip through Spain, France, and Switzerland to visit friends.
- A map of France helped me plan travel from Paris to Le Puy-en-Velay to start the Le Puy route—and helped me get back to Paris after finishing just before the Spanish border in Saint-Jean-Pied-de-Port.
- A map of western Europe helped me organize a plan B after a foot injury stopped my Camino journey.
- General orientation maps also help me plan tourist-type visits before starting a Camino journey—a great way to get over jet lag when you first arrive in Europe.

To save even more weight, you could always buy a general orientation map *after* you finish your Camino walk, or toss out the map at the trailhead before you start walking.

It's not necessarily a huge weight burden, though: my western Europe map weighs 42 grams (1.5 ounces). That's little weight to carry in exchange for having a helpful resource at hand.

Pilgrim's Credential

To stay overnight in pilgrim-only accommodations, you need a pilgrim's credential, called a *credencial del peregrino* in Spanish and a *créanciale du pèlerin* in French. It's a type of pilgrim's passport that authorizes you to use pilgrims' facilities.

This little booklet is stamped and dated every night, usually by the caretaker of the pilgrims' refuge. Many hotels, inns, and bed-and-breakfast accommodations will also stamp the credential for you. It's a good way to remember where you stayed each night, and fun to look at after you've completed your journey.

When you arrive in Santiago de Compostela, you can present your credential at the Pilgrims' Office next to the cathedral as proof of your journey. They'll translate your name into Latin and write it on a *Compostela,* a document that certifies your completed journey. This is a centuries-old tradition. To receive a *Compostela,* you must walk at least the last 100 kilometers (about 62 miles) to the city of Santiago de Compostela.

Several years ago the Pilgrims' Office started asking pilgrims to get their credential stamped twice per day if they begin their journey in Galicia—the autonomous region in northwest Spain that is home to the city of Santiago de Compostela. They hoped that this requirement would discourage those who "cheat" to get the *Compostela*—by driving a car or taking a bus or train instead of walking the last 100 kilometers to Santiago (the minimum requirement to get the *Compostela* when traveling by foot—check with the Pilgrims' Office for the requirements when cycling or riding a horse or donkey to Santiago). So if you plan to start in Galicia and would like to receive the pilgrims' *Compostela,* get one stamp at your accommodation, and another stamp from a church, town hall, or the local police along the way—every day. If you start your pilgrimage journey outside of Galicia, only one stamp per day is required. (Visit the Pilgrims' Office website, www.peregrinossantiago.es/eng/, to see if this is still their policy by the time you read this information.)

The guidebook for the route you'll walk is the best source of information on where to obtain your pilgrim's credential. You might get it at a Camino pilgrims' association office, or at a church or cathedral or their affiliated offices. Allow plenty of time if you order a credential from a pilgrims' association before leaving home— some can take as long as a month to arrive. You can find Camino associations and their website links through the Confraternity of Saint James.

Getting Your Pilgrim's Credential in Europe

I prefer to get my pilgrim's credential at a pilgrims' association office in France or Spain, where I can also get the latest information for the route. For example, at these offices I've been warned to delay my journey for a day or two due to expected severe weather. I've also been given a hand-sketched map for a recently changed section of the trail and have been told to use the paved road instead of going through the vineyards stretch of the trail if the rain doesn't let up (making the vineyards muddy and walking difficult). The pilgrims' offices also have the latest information on recently closed refuges and can tell you where there are newly opened refuges. This kind of up-to-date information is not found in guidebooks, so it's a good idea to at least occasionally stop by a pilgrims' association office along the way.

You need not be Roman Catholic to obtain a pilgrim's credential. People of any faith, or no faith, walk the Camino. The great tradition is that the Camino is open to all.

THE BACKPACK ITSELF

Where Lightweight Begins

CHAPTER 12

BACKPACK FEATURES TO CONSIDER
How to Avoid a Heavy Backpack Before You Start Packing

Heavy loads require a heavy backpack to support that weight: this means a sturdy frame, substantial hip belt, and thick padded shoulder straps.

A lighter load offers the opportunity to use a lightweight backpack: no frame, slim hip belt, and lightly padded shoulder straps.

In other words, the weight of the backpack itself plays a role in creating a lightweight backpack.

Caution

If your backpack contents weigh much more than about 11–12 percent of your body weight, you'll likely need a backpack with more structure and features to support that load. Carrying a heavy load in a backpack that has minimal features will put too much stress on your body.

Example: Heavy Backpack Versus Lightweight Backpack

Note the difference in features and weight between my first Camino backpack and the one I currently use. Both have about the same volume capacity, but the difference in weight is nearly a kilogram (about 2 pounds).

First Camino Backpack	Current Camino Backpack
Front loading (also called panel loading)	Top loading
Internal metal frame	No internal frame
Pack closes with a wide metal zipper	Pack closes with a thin drawstring
2 side pockets with metal zippers	2 mesh side pockets
2 front pockets with metal zippers	1 front pocket with plastic zipper
Durable, heavy fabric	Durable, lightweight fabric
Thick padded shoulder straps	Lightly padded shoulder straps
Thick padded hip belt	No hip belt padding
Empty backpack weight 1.4 kilograms (50 ounces)	**Empty backpack weight 587 grams (20.7 ounces)**

I loved the sturdy metal zippers, thick shoulder straps, and wide padded hip belt on my first backpack. I also loved zipping open the front of the bag to reveal all its contents at a glance. But I love carrying a lightweight backpack even more.

Finding a Proper Fit: A Backpack's Shape and Design

The first thing to look for in a backpack is a comfortable width and length for your torso. Just like a well-fitting jacket fits at the shoulders and falls to a desired length, a backpack should fit your body. Try different models to find the backpack that feels most comfortable.

Then add weight to the backpack and try it on again. Outdoor stores often provide weighted sandbags for this purpose. Fill the pack to equal at least 10 percent of your body weight, perhaps a bit more. No sandbags? Fill the pack with books, boots, or other weighty items. If the store has a scale, ask if they'll weigh the filled pack for you.

The hip belt should rest over your hip bones—some say over the navel—and should feel like it's helping to carry the load. Make sure it's adjustable.

Adjust the shoulder straps for a fine-tuned fit. With weight in the pack, you shouldn't have the feeling that you're being pulled backward. The full pack should fit snug against your back. Notice if the hip belt and shoulder straps help carry the pack weight in about equal measure.

Test the chest (sternum) strap. This feature helps to center and secure the pack, so it doesn't shift or slightly wobble from side to side as you walk. It helps keep the shoulder straps in place too. A sliding chest strap is best: you can move it up or down to where it's most comfortable and not pressing against the stuff in your shirt's pockets. Women, remember that a chest strap is not a *breast* strap. It should cross the upper chest above the breasts.

Walk around the store wearing the loaded backpack. The full pack should feel like it's a part of your body as you walk. Browse for at least an hour to get a sense of how the pack feels. Better yet: if the store offers a liberal exchange or refund policy, take it home for a serious test walk.

If your shoulders ache under the weight of the loaded backpack, with no relief after adjusting the hip belt and/or chest strap, the design or shape of the pack may not be the best for your body type. Try another model.

If you're buying online, allow plenty of time before your Camino journey. You may need to return the pack if it's not the right fit, and that back and forth takes time.

Just Enough Room: The Backpack's Volume

Backpack sizes are indicated by volume. For example, you'll see a backpack marked "40 L," which means the backpack has a volume of forty liters. Sometimes a measurement description uses cubic inches. Forty liters—the size of my backpack—equals about 2,441 cubic inches. This means the pack can hold forty liters, or 2,441 cubic inches, worth of stuff.

Are these measurements helpful? Of course not.

A recommendation: Assemble all the items you plan to carry in your backpack and place them in a trash bag. Take it to a store that sells backpacks, and try placing your filled trash bag into different backpacks. Remember to allow extra room for food and water, and don't forget the bulky sleeping bag, which is likely to be the largest item in your pack. Note the volume measurement for the backpack that best fits the sack full of your gear. Then, whether you buy a backpack in a store or online, you'll know how many liters or cubic inches you need.

Another Caution
Backpacks can be like drawers, closets, and garages.
Got extra space?
It shall be filled.

Backpack Features
Hooks and Straps

In terms of hooks and straps, the fewer the better. You'll never need to hang an ice pick from your backpack along the Camino. If you like a particular pack but it has unnecessary straps or hooks, buy the pack. Then save a few grams by cutting off the features you won't use.

Simplicity = Lightweight

Top Loading or Front Loading?

A top-loading pack almost always weighs less than a similar-size front-loading backpack. The zippers on a front-loading pack, and the extra fabric surrounding the zippers, add to the overall weight.

It's wonderful to unzip a front-loading backpack to see everything at a glance. But consider this: while you may appreciate that convenience for about fifteen minutes each day, you'll likely appreciate carrying the lighter top-loading backpack every hour you're walking the Camino.

Frame or No Frame?

I suggest a backpack without a frame, but only if your total backpack weight—including food and water—is no more than about 11 or 12 percent of your body weight.

Backpack frames, whether internal or external, are useful when carrying a heavy load. They provide a structure to help control the backpack's shape and distribute the weight. But you don't need the same structural support on the Camino that a wilderness backpacker needs for carrying all that food, a cookstove, a tent, and more.

Today, most backpack frames are internal. An internal frame is integrated into the backpack's design, and not visible—although it can usually be removed. An external frame is clearly visible on the outside of the pack.

Ventilation at the Back

Some backpacks use materials and designs to create a cooling space between the backpack and your back. While these can make the pack more comfortable, especially in hot weather, the extra materials used for this benefit add weight to the backpack itself.

Consider the tradeoff: a lighter pack that is more comfortable, or a heavier pack with ventilation features that make the pack more comfortable.

Outside Pockets

One large zippered pocket on the outside of the backpack is sufficient for carrying maps, a guidebook, and rain gear. Two side pockets work well enough for carrying water bottles and other items like a snack or sunglasses.

Outside pockets allow quick access, but keep in mind that extra material for a pocket and its zipper adds to the overall weight of the pack; mesh pockets are the lightest in weight. Overall, the fewer pockets the better.

Hydration System: Pros and Cons

Some backpacks come with a specially designed pocket inside to hold a soft-plastic collapsible water bladder called a hydration reservoir. A plastic hose with a valve at the end extends from the reservoir to hang outside the pack, allowing you to easily sip water from the reservoir without having to take your backpack off.

Some backpacks come with the reservoir and hose, while others have just the internal pocket and a slit for the hose so you can insert your own reservoir bought separately.

Reservoir Benefits
- You can drink water while walking, without having to take off your backpack to access water bottles in side pockets that may be hard to reach.
- Water weight is equally balanced in your pack.
- It's easier to avoid using disposable plastic water bottles—just refill the reservoir.
- Capacity: reservoirs for long-distance backpacking (rather than day hikes) typically hold two to three liters of water (70–100 fluid ounces). If there are few opportunities for water refills during parts of the route, you can buy bottled water to supplement your backpack hydration system. You could also avoid filling the reservoir to full capacity when it's clear that you'll have many opportunities to refill it throughout the day. Remember that water will be one of the heaviest items in your backpack—so don't carry more than you think you'll need (after a few days on the Camino, you'll know the average amount of water you'll need for each day's walk).

The Case Against Hydration Systems

Whether to use a hydration system is really a matter of personal preference. For a variety of reasons, I don't use one. I find it faster and easier to refill a water bottle than a hydration reservoir that may have to be taken out of the backpack to fit under a water faucet. Besides, handing a bartender, café owner, or restaurant worker a plastic bottle to fill (especially when he or she is busy) is one thing. Presenting the weird-looking bladder or hoisting up the entire backpack to a faucet is another.

I prefer hard plastic bottles to hold water—especially when the weather is hot—rather than the soft plastic of a polyurethane hydration system. My experience: soft plastic containers for water leave a plastic taste lingering in my mouth.

I also don't want to deal with the cleaning and maintenance of such a system while on an extended Camino journey. The kits I've seen contain more than I'd like to carry: brushes, cleaning tablets, and special plastic hooks for hanging the reservoir to dry.

I have also read that hydration systems sometimes leak, particularly around the screw cap when the bladder is squeezed—and of course the bladder would experience pressure in a fully loaded backpack (as would the owner of the backpack if he or she had to dry out a backpack full of wet gear).

On the Camino

I don't like buying water in plastic bottles—the environmental concerns about these are well known. But by refilling them again and again on the Camino, I feel better about using them. I've found them to be the lightest choice for carrying water, the most practical, the least costly, and reliably watertight.

Another option used by backpackers is a collapsible water bottle. These can be compressed when not in use to save space in the backpack, but I've read that these too can sprout leaks at the screw cap, or get punctures in the body of the bottle. Some brands could be more susceptible to problems like this, so it's a good idea to read customer reviews. Collapsible bottles are also hard to clean, and it's difficult to get them completely dry on the inside.

Some pilgrims prefer non-BPA hard plastic bottles (Bisphenol A, or BPA, is a compound used in certain plastics—and some governments and organizations have issued health warnings related to its use). Other pilgrims like to use a light metal water bottle. As always, consider the weight: a lightweight metal water bottle often weighs more than a hard plastic one.

Overall Backpack Quality: Notice the Details

After finding a proper-fitting backpack, consider the construction quality:

- Look for strong stitching at the seams.
- Look for extra fabric thickness on the bottom of the pack.
- Test for smooth zipping: even a plastic zipper on a pocket should move with ease. A stuck or off-track zipper can prevent quick access to that rain gear, possibly causing you to release a flood of colorful words while you get wet.
- Waterproof material is a bonus, but often unreliable, so you'll still need to protect your pack against the rain. (See the next section, Backpack Rain Protection.)
- The fabric of the backpack itself affects the overall weight of the pack. Avoid thick, heavy fabrics. Look for thin, high-tech, and durable fabrics.
- Sometimes quality control fails at the factory. When you find flaws in materials or construction, look at another backpack of the same model; you might find better stitching and/or smoother zipping.

Backpack Rain Protection

A wet sleeping bag or damp clothing can make your journey miserable for days. It's important to protect your pack from rain, even if it's supposedly waterproof. In the rough and tumble life of a backpack, waterproof qualities can be scraped away or worn off. Seams may not be fully taped, and zippers can also be a source of leaks.

Rain Cover

If you're wearing a rain jacket, or if you're uncertain that your poncho will keep your backpack completely dry in a downpour, use a waterproof backpack rain cover. A cover will slip on quickly and is held snug by elasticized hems. It's lightweight, and about the size of a fist when compressed into its little stuff sack.

If you bring a sleeping pad, make sure the rain cover is large enough to cover the pad too. If the sleeping pad is attached horizontally to the top or the bottom of your backpack, it might be difficult to stretch the rain cover so it fits both the backpack and the sleeping pad. Try strapping the sleeping pad vertically on the side of your backpack—so it's snug lengthwise against one side of the pack.

SLEEPING PADS STRAPPED TO THE SIDES OF PILGRIMS' BACKPACKS AS THEY LEAVE SAINT-JEAN-PIED-DE-PORT, FRANCE, ON THE CAMINO FRANCÉS ROUTE (I WONDER IF THAT HAT MADE IT TO SANTIAGO)

Inside-the-Backpack Liner

A liner inside the backpack surrounds all the gear inside the pack.

Even if you're confident of your backpack's waterproofness, and even though you're using a rain cover, I still recommend using a waterproof liner inside the pack as well for final assurance. This is especially important if you're carrying a down-filled sleeping bag, because down loses its insulating qualities when it gets wet.

The cheapest and lightest option for a liner is a large plastic trash bag. No need to spend twenty to thirty euros on a backpack liner when the trash sack is easy to get, easy to use, and very effective. You may need to try a different size or two to get the right fit—start with any trash bags you might have at home. The bag doesn't need to fit the backpack perfectly: the goal is to simply surround the gear inside your backpack. I use a size that slightly overlaps the top of my backpack (which is a top-loading pack). I twist the extra material to seal the trash sack. My backpack's top flap then covers the twisted top of the trash bag.

———————

Now let's look at how to organize the contents within your backpack.

CHAPTER 13

ORGANIZING AND PACKING YOUR BACKPACK
Suggested Weight Distribution and Tips for a Tidy Pack

It's much easier to live out of a backpack when its contents are well organized. Try to organize backpack contents by category:

- Store blister treatments with the first aid kit.
- Combine all toiletry items.
- Put socks with underwear.
- Keep all rain gear in one bag.
- Stash a pocketknife and spoon in the food bag.

Keep categorized items in bags or sacks, using drawstrings to secure the contents. Use whatever size is needed for each category of items, and choose different colors for easy identification.

Although sacks or bags are not essential, most backpackers find them very helpful. After assembling your gear into categories, you'll know how many bags to get and in what sizes.

Types of Sacks and Bags

Compression sacks squeeze the air out of items to make them as small as possible, creating more space inside the backpack. Although compression sacks work well, especially for bulky sleeping bags, the straps and buckles used to cinch the sack tight do add extra weight. A lighter option, such as a stuff sack, can also compress fluffy things.

Stuff sacks are lighter than compression sacks because they use a drawcord, instead of straps and buckles, to secure contents. They're available in a variety of fabrics, such as siliconized fabric for waterproofness or mesh fabric for visibility (great for storing clothes).

Ditty bags or sacks are smaller stuff sacks. If you want to protect a camera or mobile phone, a waterproof ditty bag works well. Or group together various small items—a snack bar, a box of mints, lip balm, a vial of sunscreen—in one ditty sack and store it in the backpack's outside pocket for quick access.

Ziplock bags are great for seeing contents at a glance. Current airport security guidelines require using a quart-size ziplock bag for liquids, so you'll need at least one anyway if you're flying to France or Spain. They're also great for keeping maps and guidebook pages dry. I use a ziplock bag to separate emergency food from the other contents in my food bag. A ziplock bag could also be used to hold your money belt while showering in a pilgrims' refuge, instead of leaving valuables somewhere you can't keep an eye on them.

Ordinary plastic bags can be useful, but choose the least crinkly type you can find: fellow pilgrims might be sleeping while you rummage through your backpack. Recycled-plastic shopping bags are often the least noisy choice. I use a "quiet" shopping bag from a clothing store to hold my alternate footwear and dirty laundry. A thin cellophane bag holds all my rain gear, which helps prevent the waterproof repellent from being scraped off the fabric when I pull the rain gear out of my backpack.

Accessory pockets or pouches clip onto a backpack's hip belt. Don't forget to weigh them, because they still count as weight being carried. I once tried two clip-on pouches, but soon mailed them home. They're awkward, especially when taking off the backpack. Keeping small miscellaneous items in a pants pocket or in a ditty bag kept in the backpack's side pocket works better. Also, many backpacks now have small side pockets built into the backpack's hip belt, perfect for holding the little things.

How to Pack
Balance

Walking with an out-of-balance backpack is like carrying two grocery sacks, one heavier than the other, for many kilometers. That imbalance could eventually cause strain or injury on the back, hips, knees, or feet.

Be sure that the load is spread equally across the body. Shift items inside the backpack and in the side pockets so the pack doesn't tilt to one side while you walk. It should also feel like the weight of the pack is pushing you forward, rather than pulling you back. Keep the heaviest items toward the top and against your back. That helps prevent the shoulders from straining backward from the weight.

Aim for the overall feeling that the backpack is a comfortable part of your body, worn without much thought.

Access

Keep what you'll need for the day's walk close at hand: water, food, rain gear, sunscreen, sunglasses, guidebook, and maps. If you take a sleeping pad, carry it strapped to the outside of your backpack. Then it's accessible for breaks, lunch, or an afternoon siesta.

Suggested Weight Distribution

Easy-Access Food Bag
(for snacks and lunch)

Heavy

Medium

Light

Sleeping Bag

Hydration System
(or carry water bottles in the outside side pockets)

Easy-Access Rain Gear
(outside front pocket)

Buying Camino Gear

CHAPTER 14

SHOPPING ADVICE:
Including Types of Outdoor-Gear Fabrics and a Few Favorites

Where to Shop

Look for Camino gear at travel, outdoor, and/or sporting-goods stores. If you're shopping online, be sure the company offers a liberal exchange policy. This especially pertains to footwear. It's difficult to know how comfortable footwear is until it's been tested by walking several kilometers with a fully loaded backpack.

Google is helpful when searching for specific items, such as a backpacker's towel or a backpacker's first aid kit. A search under the general category of "lightweight backpacking gear" will bring up a variety of online and local bricks-and-mortar stores that carry these types of items.

Getting Gear Advice from Experienced Pilgrims

It can be overwhelming to sort through the many choices for backpacking gear. Knowing what others use often provides a shopping shortcut.

Before buying anything, visit pilgrims' websites (a Google search will help you find the most up-to-date websites, and then you can click on their links to find more Camino-related websites). Many experienced pilgrims have even posted their Camino packing lists on their websites. Pay attention to the brand names or models of specific backpacking items that are mentioned by these experienced pilgrims. (Check the dates of the posts so you know if you're getting the latest information.) If you're not finding what you need to know, post a question yourself on the Camino pilgrimage forums or send an email to an experienced pilgrim through their website.

I'd recommend starting at the following English-language resource sites.

Confraternity of Saint James (www.csj.org.uk) doesn't have a pilgrims' forum, but they offer helpful links to additional information on planning your Camino pilgrimage.

Other general-information sites, with pilgrims' forums for questions and answers about the Camino pilgrimage, are www. caminodesantiago.me and www.caminodesantiago.me.uk.

Tip: Do a search on Google for "[item name, brand name, or trademark] problem." That will guide you to discussions that offer a good starting point to research the quality of a particular brand, piece of gear, or type of fabric.

Where the Author Shops

Some of my gear comes from local resources, but some of it I buy from companies that sell internationally. I've been pleased with the following items and companies. I don't mention specific model names unless the item seems to be a product that the company continues to sell over the years. That's because it's not unusual for backpacking gear to be changed slightly, then renamed for a new product launch—or discontinued altogether.

GoLite
www.golite.com

- Jam Pack backpack
- Rain jacket
- Long-sleeve silk T-shirt

GoLite also sells sleeping bags and other well-made lightweight gear.

Western Mountaineering
www.westernmountaineering.com

I love Western Mountaineering's Flight Series Vest. They have another vest, called the Flash Vest, that is even more lightweight: average total weight is about 99 grams (3.5 ounces). The Flash Vest weighs less than the Flight Series because it doesn't have pockets or a collar.

Rick Steves
www.ricksteves.com

- Water-resistant paper map of western Europe, includes rail transportation information
- Money belt

The Rick Steves store carries a variety of travel-related items. Email to find out if they deliver to your country (they process orders outside the U.S. differently).

J. R. Liggett's
www.jrliggett.com

Multipurpose body soap, shampoo, and laundry soap in an all-in-one bar. Don't let the laundry-soap part scare you: it's a very mild soap. There is a fragrance-free option.

Feet Relief
www.feetrelief.com

I buy toe gel caps from this company. They also carry a wide variety of other foot-care products. It's not easy to find the toe gel caps from the main page. Click on "Products" at the top of the home page, then scroll down to "Feet Relief," and finally click on the link "Toe Caps & More."

Other Suppliers

I've also been happy with footwear, clothing, and other backpacking gear from REI (www.rei.com), hiking pants and shirts from ExOfficio (www.exofficio.com), and alternate footwear from Crocs (www.crocs.com). These companies have a limited sales range outside of North America; contact them for details.

Fabrics for Outdoor Clothing and Gear

It's helpful to know something about the fabrics used in outdoor clothing and other gear like sleeping bags, although one could write an encyclopedia on this topic alone.

Serious backpackers frequently debate the best fabric choices for their gear. Look for discussions in lightweight-backpacking books or magazines or on websites that provide articles and/or reviews on outdoor gear. Read comments from the readers of those reviews too, as they might share their own experiences about specific gear or clothing. Google "lightweight backpacking magazines" to find many sites to choose from.

If you are (or want to be) fabric obsessed, visit www.fabriclink.com. Click "Trademark" on the left side of the website's home page to access the Alphabetical Trademark/Brand Name Index. This is a descriptive list of almost 200 fabrics by trademark name, many of which you'll see on labels for outdoor clothing and sleeping bags, such as Gore-Tex and Polartec. This list shows every trademarked variation for those two names and many others.

I don't need so much detail; it's good enough for me to know that Gore-Tex has provided me with decent rain protection for years, along with some degree of breathability in the garment fabric or footwear. I also find it good enough to know that the Polartec umbrella term, and whatever their latest generation of that substance, provides a decent synthetic insulation in clothing or sleeping bags when natural down fill is too expensive.

Remember that many of the established and trademarked fabric names have rivals worth considering. New products and technologies are invented and released into the marketplace every year. As mentioned earlier, you can do a Google search to learn more about the quality of any product with an unfamiliar name.

General Fabric Qualities

Most people are familiar with natural fabrics, such as cotton, wool, or silk. These fabrics are often blended with synthetic materials in backpack clothing or gear. Combining the much-loved properties of natural fabrics with fabric technologies can alleviate some of the drawbacks of the natural fibers and improve the performance of an outdoor garment—for example, through enhanced wicking properties and ease of care.

Other products are made entirely of synthetic materials, including some old standbys such as nylon. New synthetics are frequently invented, and many of them are especially targeted for backpackers, travelers, and those who participate in active sports.

Natural Fabrics in Outdoor Clothing

Cotton holds moisture and takes a long time to dry. Even in cold weather you're likely to perspire, and a constantly wet cotton T-shirt or even cotton pants next to your skin will make you feel miserable. Pure cotton is also heavier in weight than other fabric choices. Not recommended.

Silk is lightweight, warm for its weight, and insulating, and has better wicking properties than cotton. Caution: silk items might have fussy wash-and-dry instructions. This is less of a concern if you choose silk blended with a synthetic fiber.

Microweight merino wool is lightweight and less bulky than other wools. It's also less likely to retain odors than other fabrics, and is more durable than cotton or silk. Some have reported that microweight merino wool is even comfortable to wear in hot weather. Use caution when drying a merino wool garment in a hot dryer; some brands might shrink. Read care labels and choose a dryer-friendly merino wool (it does exist) when possible.

Down Feathers provide the best warmth-to-weight ratio. And down compresses well, so it takes up less space in the backpack. But a caution: down fill provides no insulation when wet. It's especially not recommended for your outermost layer.

Synthetic Fabrics in Outdoor Clothing

One of the biggest advantages of synthetic fabrics is that they dry quickly: it's easy to wash them in the evening and find them perfectly dry by morning (synthetics blended with natural fabrics can also dry fairly quickly, but it ultimately depends on the weight of the fabric).

Polypropylene (polypro), polyester, MTS 2, and Capilene are some of the most common fabrics that provide wicking and are quick drying. They're often used for inner-layer or mild-weather garments such as underwear, T-shirts, and turtlenecks.

Nylon is frequently used in hiking pants and shirts. My experience is that nylon should be blended with another fabric that can eliminate static cling. I once had to return a pair of 100 percent nylon hiking pants because they stuck uncomfortably to my legs and wouldn't let go!

Polar fleece or microfleece (commonly referred to simply as fleece) is a lightweight insulator. Among Camino pilgrims it's often the fabric of choice for jackets, hats, and gloves. It comes in a variety of thicknesses, so be careful of the weight—and bulk. As mentioned earlier, a 100-weight fleece is usually sufficient for most people while hiking. But if you tend to get cold easily, consider the mid-weight category of thickness: 200-weight. A heavyweight fleece (300-weight) would likely be too warm. Avoid the windproof fleece—it likely has a laminate in the fabric that will diminish the breathability of the fleece.

Microfiber is known for its softness, durability, absorption, and wicking abilities, and tends to have some water repellency. A popular alternative to cotton for many athletic types, it's often used in undergarments too.

Sleeping Bag Fills

Synthetic fills for sleeping bags have steadily improved, to the point that they now rival the warmth-to-weight ratio of down feathers. Bags made with synthetic fill are often less expensive than those with down fill, and unlike down, synthetic fill retains some warmth if it gets wet. Specially treated polyester microfiber, such as the PrimaLoft brand (also used in insulation layers of clothing), has had good reviews.

Outdoor-Gear Shopping Tips for Women

Women hike just like men do. So why are there women's trekking poles? Women have a back, hips, and shoulders, as do men; why are there women's backpacks? Why are there men's and women's sleeping bags?

The explanation is simple: marketing. One quick glance at a crowd of people anywhere in the world shows that body types vary among men just as much as they do among women. Find what's right for you and your body, not what marketing ploys tell you to buy. Avoid marketing techniques that overlook practicality, comfort, and function. Avoid cute and stylish. Think practical, and think unisex. As they should, most pilgrims care about the performance of their clothing or gear, not how fashionable they look.

Fit matters too. Notice how more material is sometimes invested in men's clothing than women's, even for what is essentially the same garment. Men rarely wear short or tight-fitting outdoor clothing. Loose and baggy is best for all human bodies on the Camino. It's perfect for comfort, and for layering.

Women might even save money by shopping in the men's section. Fashion-conscious women's outdoor clothing (skimpier cuts and "feminine" colors) often costs more than similar-functioning clothing made for men. I've sometimes noticed that men's clothing is even made from better-quality fabrics and has better features, like multiple pockets large enough to carry more than just a tube of lipstick.

I chose a men's waterproof watch because it allows me to see the time without using my reading glasses (women's sport watches are usually smaller). I discovered that the difference between a "male" first aid kit and one for women was simply a few pills for PMS. After an extensive and frustrating search, a female friend finally found that a pair of men's hiking pants fit better than any of the women's pants she'd been trying on. They even looked like women's hiking pants—because a woman was wearing them.

Clothing needs are essentially the same for men and women on the Camino—we're all walking upon the same earth and under the same ever-changing skies—so buy whatever works for you.

Beware the Word *Lightweight*

Finally, be careful when you see the word *lightweight* while shopping. Lightweight backpacking is the latest trend, and marketing experts know it.

Many backpacks, for example, are now advertised as lightweight due to this recent trend. But I saw one "lightweight" pack that weighed about 2 kilograms (more than 4 pounds)—empty. That's not even close to a lightweight backpack (mine weighs just over a half kilo).

Weigh and compare everything. Judge for yourself if something is lightweight or not.

———————

Reading these tips and lists might have some of you worried about how much all of this gear is going to cost. Never fear: the Camino is for everyone, and there are plenty of ways to save money as you prepare your lightweight backpack.

CHAPTER 15

FOR LIMITED BUDGETS
How to Save Money on Backpacking Gear

During the 1955 hiking season, a woman walked 3,489 kilometers (2,168 miles) alone on the Appalachian Trail on the East Coast of the United States. Her name was Emma Rowena Gatewood, but everyone called her Grandma Gatewood. At the time she was sixty-seven years old; married to a farmer, she was the mother of eleven children and had twenty-three grandchildren. According to hikers' lore, she hiked in tennis shoes and used a handmade bag slung over her shoulder to carry cans of tuna fish, an army blanket, a raincoat, and a plastic shower curtain.

Grandma Gatewood (1887–1973) last hiked the Appalachian Trail at age seventy-six. Her story tells us this: it's your spirit, not what you carry or what you wear, that will see you through. If your spirit harbors Camino dreams, go. Don't worry if you don't have the resources to gather all the "right" gear. Just take whatever you need that you have at home. The tips in this chapter will help you make the most of a limited budget.

Follow the Lightweight Packing Principle

The only items I bought before my first Camino journey were boots and socks. I had no awareness of lightweight backpacking principles. I even wore jeans. (Don't tell anyone about that: jeans are the worst choice for the Camino, and my face turns pink just thinking about it.)

But, since the weight of your backpack (and the comfort of your footwear) will largely determine your health and happiness on the Camino, it's important to follow the lightweight backpacking principles discussed in this book—even when you're on a budget. Again, the key is to weigh everything and to choose the lightest options. Get as close as you can to that goal of a backpack that weighs about 10 percent of your body weight.

With creativity and imagination you can organize a Camino backpack that's both inexpensive and lightweight—remember Grandma Gatewood's shower curtain when you need inspiration. That was likely a multi-purpose item, and I can imagine her using it as a poncho, as a ground cloth to sleep on (the Appalachian Trail requires taking camping equipment) and to sit on while she ate her tuna fish for lunch—and maybe dinner too.

Footwear Advice

Grandma Gatewood almost certainly had tough feet, hiking so many miles in sneakers. I wonder how she handled having wet feet for hours, perhaps days. Did she get blisters? After all, walking with wet socks and shoes is practically guaranteed to cause blisters for most people.

When choosing your footwear, plan on rain and even deep mud on the trail. Some Camino routes also require walking for long distances on paved roads—for many people, this surface causes their feet the most problems. Having shoes with adequate soles will help protect your feet.

My strongest recommendation for someone with a limited budget is this: invest in good footwear. Your spirit will see you through to Santiago, but your feet will carry you there.

Rain Gear Advice

It's not just your stuff that can get wet on the Camino; spirits can be dampened too. Here's another strong recommendation: invest in effective rain gear.

A poncho could be the least expensive option. It might also be more effective than an inexpensive non-breathable jacket that will likely cause overheating and excessive perspiration when walking in the rain.

If you prefer a jacket, but you can only afford one made from a non-breathable fabric, get a size much larger than normal. The bigger and baggier the better, for more ventilation. Especially if the jacket is made with a soft plastic material, you could find condensation forming on the inside of the jacket as you warm up from walking. Then you'll get wet from the inside.

To prevent their legs from getting wet, some backpackers take an extra-large trash bag, cut it open at the sealed end, and wear it over their shorts as a type of waterproof kilt, held up by their backpack's hip belt.

Legs can get cold under the plastic kilt, though, so other budget backpackers have taken large trash bags, cut them to the shape of rain chaps, and then sealed them with duct tape. Those can then be worn over hiking pants.

Using Old or Abused Rain Gear

I first realized that rain gear has a shelf life when a pair of rain pants failed after having provided perfect protection throughout the previous year's Camino journey. The waterproofing properties had simply worn off the fabric. I stopped my walk that day in a small French town, and was lucky to find a shop that actually sold rain pants.

If you have doubts about your old rain gear (you can test it at home in the shower), buy waterproof spray at an outdoor store to extend the waterproof life of the garment. Or, take it to a dry cleaner that provides waterproofing treatment.

Money-Saving Tips
Use What You Already Have

- Consider every item and ask, "How can I make this lighter?" Cut things to their practical essence.
- Take the internal frame out of an old backpack, or remove a metal external frame. Cut off unnecessary straps, buckles, and pockets. Remove padding from the hip belt and shoulder straps. If your pack's contents are truly lightweight, you won't need that padding.
- Take an old sleeping bag and cut it to the shape of a mummy bag, then re-sew the seams. Shorten the length, if that length is more than your body needs.

- Trim a threadbare old towel to the minimal size needed to dry yourself after a shower. Or use a dishcloth as a towel.
- Choose your most lightweight clothing. Synthetics dry fast and weigh the least. Cotton clothing is heavy and takes forever to dry in damp conditions. Wool can be bulky and heavy. Adding additional thin clothing layers could be more lightweight and less bulky in your backpack than one thicker item.
- Cut pants off at the calf or the knee for a pair of capris. Roll up the cuffs, and you won't need to bother sewing a hem.
- Women: cross the aisle and look in the men's department. Sometimes things are less expensive there.
- Make your own first aid kit, and store the items in a ziplock bag. Look at the contents of backpacker's first aid kits to know what to take. (Google "backpacker's first aid kit" to find a list of items for a small first aid kit.)
- Use a large plastic trash sack to cover your backpack in the rain instead of buying a rain cover.

Buy Used Gear

- Avid backpackers are constantly updating their gear. Look for classified ads in backpacking magazines or in your local newspaper and on bulletin boards at outdoor stores. Go to the Backpacking Light website (www.backpackinglight.com) to see what you can find under "Used Gear."
- Search websites like eBay, Craigslist, and Amazon to find used backpacks, boots, hiking clothes, and other gear for sale.
- Check outdoor stores to see if they have sales on returned items or discontinued brands and models of backpacking gear.
- Ask friends or family if they have any backpacking gear you can buy or borrow from them.

Consider the Least Expensive Items

Inexpensive sometimes means less material, thus less weight—and cheaper items could be just as good, or better, than expensive options. An example: I once needed new socks while walking the Camino in Spain. At the time, my only choice was a pair of cheap, thin men's socks from a small village shop. I thought they'd work well enough until I could get to a shop in a larger town or city.

But those socks turned out to be fantastic, and they made me question why I was buying expensive "backpacking" socks. Although there are good reasons to invest in a pair of high-quality socks (especially for walking on paved roads), thin socks can work well enough on certain terrain (particularly off-road).

Make Your Own Gear

Aspiring pilgrims with limited budgets can also sew their own backpack, rain gear, stuff sacks, sleeping bag, and other items.

I already mentioned that I once made rain chaps, but neglected to use the correct material (I should have used a waterproof, rather than water-repellent, fabric). If you want to make your own rain gear, keep my error in mind when choosing materials.

Resources

You can also purchase backpacking gear kits that come with all the materials and instructions you'll need to make your own. Ray Jardine, an American who has experimented for years with techniques for lightweight backpacking, sells kits through his website, www.rayjardine.com. He's also the author of *Trail Life: Lightweight Backpacking*. Both the book and the website provide resources for making your own lightweight gear. Jardine's focus is wilderness backpacking, but his philosophy and techniques can be applied to Camino journeys too.

Another resource for buying outdoor-gear fabrics, patterns, fasteners, zippers, and more is Quest Outfitters (www.questoutfitters.com).

Too Cheap: Don't Do This

One night at a pilgrims' refuge, in a room with about twenty pilgrims all eager for a good night's sleep, two women unfurled space blankets on top of their bunk beds.

Lights out. Then: crinkle, crinkle, crinkle. Giggle, giggle, giggle. All night long (or so it seemed). The rest of the pilgrims woke up cranky. The two women? Gone—apparently they'd taken off in the wee hours. I'm guessing it was their first and last night on the Camino.

Space blankets, in theory, are a great idea: They're lightweight! They're inexpensive! Should they be used on the Camino? No!

Summary: Everything Worn and Carried on the Camino

CHAPTER 16

EXAMPLE CAMINO PACK LIST
Walking Clothes, Pocket Contents, Backpack Contents—and the Weight of Each Item

This list should serve only as a starting point for you to compose your own list. For the same reason that my home is different from your home, your backpack and its contents will be different from mine, and from anybody else's. The definitive Camino pack list doesn't exist.

Of course, the total weight of my backpack will also be different from your final weight tally. My clothing size is probably not the same as yours. You may prefer a bottle of soap instead of a bar. You might prefer a larger pack towel, and a different type of alternate footwear.

Total Weight for Everything Carried in the Example Backpack
7763 grams (7.76 kilograms) or 273.64 ounces (17.1 pounds)
The total weight includes food and water, but does not include walking clothes or pocket contents.

The key principle is to set your backpack's total weight goal to about 10 percent of your body weight. Don't fret if it's 11 percent or even 12 percent. But make sure that the number includes the weight of food and water, which is by far the single heaviest category.

Walking Clothes (for a pleasant-weather day)
Total: 1698 grams (1.7 kilograms) or 59.7 ounces (3.7 pounds)

- **Hiking pants**
313 grams (11.0 ounces)

- **Long-sleeve shirt**
193 grams (6.8 ounces)

- **Socks**
69 grams (2.4 ounces)

- **Underpants**
40 grams (1.4 ounces)

- **Waterproof wristwatch**
41 grams (1.4 ounces)

- **Money belt**
75 grams (2.6 ounces)

- **Bucket hat**
60 grams (2.1 ounces)

- **Mid-weight hiking boots**
907 grams (32.0 ounces)

Pocket Contents (while walking)

Total: 637 grams (0.64 kilogram) or 22.3 ounces (1.39 pounds)

- **Reading glasses**
23 grams (0.8 ounce)

- **iPhone**
136 grams (4.8 ounces)

- **Pocket-size digital camera (in soft case)**
177 grams (6.2 ounces)

- **Memo pad and pen (for journaling and notes)**
65 grams (2.3 ounces)

- **Lip balm**
9 grams (0.3 ounce)

- **Gum and/or mints**
25 grams (0.9 ounce)

- **Packet of tissues**
23 grams (0.8 ounce)

- **Wallet for euro bills (weight includes 10 bills)**
39 grams (1.3 ounces)

- **Coin purse (full of coins)**
134 grams (4.7 ounces)

- **Whistle (to confuse aggressive dogs)**
6 grams (0.2 ounce)

Backpack, Sleeping Bag, Weather Protection, and Down Vest
Total: 2178 grams (2.2 kilograms) or 76.8 ounces (4.8 pounds)

- **Backpack—40-liter capacity (empty)**
587 grams (20.7 ounces)

- **Large trash sack (lines the inside of the backpack for added rain protection)**
40 grams (1.4 ounces)

- **Backpack rain cover (protects the backpack exterior from rain)**
91 grams (3.2 ounces)

- **Sleeping bag (compressed inside a stuff sack)**
723 grams (25.5 ounces)

- **Waterproof jacket**
264 grams (9.3 ounces)

- **Down vest (compressed inside a stuff sack)**
198 grams (7.0 ounces)

- **Rain pants**
224 grams (7.9 ounces)

- **Waterproof baseball hat**
51 grams (1.8 ounces)

- **Cellophane bag to hold rain gear**
Weight is negligible

Extra Clothes and Alternate Footwear
Total: 1191 grams (1.19 kilograms) or 41.9 ounces (2.6 pounds)

- **Short-sleeve T-shirt**
162 grams (5.7 ounces)

- **Long-sleeve T-shirt**
75 grams (2.6 ounces)

- **Long underwear (bottoms)**
186 grams (6.6 ounces)

- **Extra pair of pants (capris)**
266 grams (9.4 ounces)

- **Extra hiking socks (two pairs)**
138 grams (4.8 ounces)

- **Extra underpants (two pairs)**
80 grams (2.8 ounces)

- **Crocs (alternate footwear)**
252 grams (8.9 ounces)

- **Mesh sack (to hold extra clothes)**
26 grams (0.9 ounce)

- **Recycled-plastic bag (to hold Crocs and/or dirty laundry)**
6 grams (0.2 ounce)

Toiletries

Total: 414 grams (0.41 kilogram) or 14.7 ounces (0.92 pound)

- **Toothbrush (travel size)**

13 grams (0.5 ounce)

- **Toothpaste (travel size)**

28 grams (1.0 ounce)

- **Dental floss (travel size)**

5 grams (0.2 ounce)

- **Deodorant stick (travel size)**

66 grams (2.3 ounces)

- **J. R. Liggett's Soap Bar (mild soap for hair, body, and clothes)**

99 grams (3.5 ounces)

- **Comb**

11 grams (0.4 ounce)

- **Microfiber pack towel**

58 grams (2.0 ounces)

- **Microfiber face cloth**

6 grams (0.2 ounce)

- **Toilet paper (travel-size roll—55 sheets)**

30 grams (1.1 ounces)

- **Pads or tampons (only a few—can buy more along the way)**

41 grams (1.4 ounces)

- **Toenail clippers**

47 grams (1.7 ounces)

- **Ziplock plastic bag (to hold toiletries)**

10 grams (0.4 ounce)

Water, Food, and Utensils
Total: 2985 grams (2.99 kilograms) or 105.14 ounces (6.6 pounds)

- **2 liters of water (depending on water access during each day's walk, 1 liter of water may suffice)**

2000 grams (70.54 ounces)

- **1 banana, apple, or orange (average weight for one piece of fruit)**

200 grams (7 ounces)

- **Bread and cheese (light lunch)**

454 grams (16 ounces)

- **Bag of almonds (snack)**

130 grams (4.6 ounces)

- **Emergency Food:**

- **1 energy bar**

53 grams (1.8 ounces)

- **2 tea bags**

6 grams (0.02 ounce)

- **1 packet instant soup**

20 grams (0.7 ounce)

- **Utensils and Food Bag:**

- **Small spoon**

17 grams (0.06 ounce)

- **Pocketknife**

36 grams (1.3 ounces)

- **Ziplock plastic bag (to hold emergency food items)**

10 grams (0.4 ounce)

- **Food bag (to hold all food and utensils)**

59 grams (2 ounces)

First Aid, Blister Care, and Other Small Items
Total: 476 grams (0.48 kilogram) or 16.9 ounces (1.06 pounds)

- **Backpacker's first aid kit (including small scissors)**
95 grams (3.4 ounces)

- **Gentle paper tape (helps prevent blisters)**
40 grams (1.4 ounces)

- **Compeed and toe gel caps (to cover blisters)**
40 grams (1.4 ounces)

- **Aspirin (travel size)**
13 grams (0.5 ounce)

- **Hand-sanitizer spray (travel size)**
29 grams (1.0 ounce)

- **Earplugs**
2 grams (0.1 ounce)

- **Bandana**
29 grams (1.0 ounce)

- **Extra pair of eyeglasses**
23 grams (0.8 ounce)

- **Sunglasses (in lightweight carrying case)**
90 grams (3.2 ounces)

- **Sunscreen (in small plastic container)**
96 grams (3.4 ounces)

- **1 clothespin**
9 grams (0.3 ounce)

- **Ziplock plastic bag (to hold first aid and blister-care items)**
10 grams (0.4 ounce)

Maps, Guidebook, Journal, and Pilgrim's Credential
Total: 270 grams (0.27 kilogram) or 9.5 ounces (0.6 pound)

- **Route maps**

28 grams (1.0 ounce)

- **General orientation map (of western Europe)**

42 grams (1.5 ounces)

- **Guidebook (with nonessential pages ripped out and page margins trimmed)**

134 grams (4.7 ounces)

- **Pilgrim's credential**

21 grams (0.7 ounce)

- **2 extra pocket memo pads (for journaling and notes)**

35 grams (1.2 ounces)

- **Ziplock plastic bag (for holding the above items)**

10 grams (0.4 ounce)

Tech Gear, and a Pocket Pack

Total: 249 grams (0.25 kilogram) or 8.7 ounces (0.5 pound)

Note: Mobile phone and camera are listed earlier in Pocket Contents list.

- **iPhone charger**

40 grams (1.4 ounces)

- **Camera-battery charger**

69 grams (2.4 ounces)

- **Adapter plug**

46 grams (1.6 ounces)

- **Earbuds**

37 grams (1.3 ounces)

- **Pocket pack (a mini-backpack)**

57 grams (2.0 ounces)

Other Potential Items to Add to a Camino Pack List

Depending on the route or the time of year that I'm walking the Camino, sometimes I'll take certain items that are not listed in the example pack list (these items are not included in the "Total Weight for Everything Carried in the Example Backpack").

- **Rainproof gloves**
77 grams (2.7 ounces)

- **Fleece ear band**
23 grams (0.8 ounce)

- **Fleece Sherpa-style hat**
54 grams (1.9 ounces)

- **French or Spanish pocket-size language dictionary**
116 grams (4.1 ounces)

- **Blue foam sleeping pad (trimmed to save weight)**
130 grams (4.6 ounces)

- **Extra bandana**
29 grams (1.0 ounce)

- **1 baggy pair of socks (for cold feet while sleeping)**
62 grams (2.1 ounces)

- **Soluble micro-ground coffee (individual packets; weight is for 12 cups)**
46 grams (1.6 ounces)

CHAPTER 17

WALKING AIDS FOR STABILITY AND BALANCE
Sticks, Poles, Staffs, and Canes

Some pilgrims use a walking stick or a large wood staff on the Camino, while others use a cane—a French woman I met loved using her deceased father's sturdy bamboo cane. But many pilgrims prefer high-tech trekking poles, and it's not unusual to see some pilgrims walking with two of these poles. Walking aids on the Camino are used primarily for stability and balance, but also for protection—particularly against pesky dogs.

THESE DOGS DIDN'T BOTHER ME, BUT I HEARD LATER THAT ONE OF THESE SCOUNDRELS BIT A DUTCH WOMAN ON THE BACK OF HER LEG (DOGS LYING WHERE THE LEPUY AND VÉZELAY ROUTES MEET—A SPOT THOUSANDS OF PILGRIMS SAFELY PASS BY EACH YEAR).

Pilgrim Stories

You never know when a walking aid will come in handy. One spring day I wanted to catch up to a Swiss friend on the Camino. He wasn't that far ahead, but I thought I would take a shortcut by crossing a farmer's freshly plowed field. I didn't think I'd disturb anything, since the field had only large chunks of reddish-brown mud, and it was clear that no seeds had been planted yet. But by the time I had nearly reached the very muddy middle of the field, I realized my folly—and it was too late to go back. After every step I had to scrape slabs of mud off my boots with my walking stick. And as I walked, the walking stick saved me from plunging headfirst into the gooey field. So you can see how a walking aid is sometimes quite helpful. As is thinking ahead about certain situations . . .

Of course you can choose to not use a walking aid. The only way to know your preference is to try the various options before you leave home. Try them on slippery, muddy, rocky trails. Uphill, and down steep hills. On paved roads, where you don't really need one. (It bothers some people, but I don't mind the rhythmic tap, tap, tap on pavement. It goes well with my horrible singing.)

You could wait to buy a walking aid until you get to France or Spain and bring it home after you finish the Camino. My retired wooden friends stand quietly in a corner of my home. Along with a scallop shell (more on this in the next chapter), my walking aids are the enduring souvenirs from each journey. A glance at them reminds me of my Camino journeys and the fact that I can walk quite far in all sorts of terrain and in various weather conditions—which prompts me to stop being so lazy and get out for a walk!

It's easy to find walking aids in France or Spain. I've seen walking sticks and staffs in tourist shops and department stores, and even in a leather-goods store. (That staff was a work of art: lacquered wood with an exotic gnarl on top.)

I once bought an artisan-carved walking cane with Basque symbols burned into the wood. It caught my eye at a French sport shop in Saint-Jean-Pied-de-Port, where it stood au naturel next to the metal trekking poles. It's become my favorite walking aid of all, since I prefer wood over metal and because it's easy to handle while traveling to and from the Camino routes.

Walking Stick
Spanish = *bastón*
French = *bâton de marche*

Metal Trekking Poles or Staff

Typically made of carbon, aluminum, or sometimes a hybrid of the two, high-tech trekking poles can provide both strength and lightness for hikers and backpackers. Many pilgrims appreciate features such as cork or foam grips, adjustable wrist straps, ergonomic design, or a camera mount. Most trekking poles are collapsible and thus easy to carry in a backpack when they're not in use.

But they're not perfect. I once tried a collapsible walking staff and found that the tip frequently got stuck in mud, or between rocks, pulling the bottom section apart from the upper part of the staff. The consequence was that I almost lost my balance on several steep downhills. And, I know a Dutch pilgrim who broke her arm in a fall. She suspects the break would not have happened if she hadn't had trekking poles strapped to her wrists during the tumble.

Many pilgrims, however, like the collapsible feature of the metal walking aids. That provides an option to put them away in your backpack when they're not really needed—like on the long and flat stretches of the Camino Francés route in Spain, for example. It's really a matter of personal preference: some pilgrims use them all the time; others use them only to help prevent stress on their knees when they're on the steepest downhill parts of the trails.

Wooden Walking Stick, Staff, or Cane

A disadvantage of a wooden walking aid is its inflexibility. It can't collapse to fit into a backpack like a metal one can.

A wooden walking aid will cost less than its metal counterpart—unless it's made by an artist or craftsperson, in which case the price is justifiably higher.

A simple walking stick, bought from a tourist shop at or near a popular Camino starting point, is usually the best bargain.

Replacing the Wrist Strap

If you do buy an inexpensive walking stick or staff, consider replacing the thin cord that serves as a wrist strap. It won't provide real support, and it could be uncomfortable.

A French Canadian pilgrim replaced the thin wrist-strap cord on my first Camino walking stick. He bought leather strips from a local French cobbler and, after fixing his own walking stick, offered to fix mine with the leftover leather.

Since then, I take a flexible leather strip from home when I plan to buy an inexpensive wooden walking staff along the Camino.

A strip of leather a little less than two centimeters wide (about three-quarters of an inch) works well—and is about the maximum thickness that will squeeze into the pre-drilled hole of an inexpensive walking stick.

As for length, about 30.5 centimeters (just over a foot) works well for my small hands. Consider taking a longer length to ensure there's enough room for your hands. You can always use a knife to cut off any extra length you don't need.

Airports and Walking Aids as "Weapons"

Recently, I've used a walking cane instead of a walking stick or staff, primarily because of increasingly strict airport security. It's just too difficult to get a walking stick or staff through security now.

And it's sometimes impossible: I met a woman at the Madrid airport in Spain who had to surrender her beloved Camino walking stick to airport security officials. She was quite sad about leaving it behind, which I can understand: a wooden walking stick becomes a companion of sorts on the Camino. I've never heard of anyone feeling sentimental about their metal trekking poles, though. Perhaps a bit of the artisan's creative spirit lingers in a wooden walking stick. Or maybe it's because the wood was once alive, unlike metal.

If necessary, I'll use lies and deception to get my Basque walking cane through airport security. My latest strategy is to try to look old (which becomes easier by the day) and to limp a bit to make the cane seem legitimate. Who'd take a cane away from an old lady?

So far, the strategy has worked. Barely. The last time I used that scheme in Spain I had to grab at every Spanish word in my head to argue that my cane was urgently needed. A uniformed young man, afraid tears were next, finally let me limp away.

Another, less emotional option: check in your walking stick with the airline. Then hope it arrives back home with you.

(Airport security has tightened in all countries, not just Spain. One could experience the same difficulties anywhere.)

———————

In the next chapter we'll look at two additional items that are traditionally carried on a Camino pilgrimage. Don't worry: they're both tiny.

CHAPTER 18

PILGRIM TRADITIONS:
A Stone and a Shell

A friend once asked whether Camino pilgrims ever carry something that has no purpose other than to anchor themselves (as she put it) to their pilgrimage adventure. The answer is yes: pilgrims often take something to enhance their personal journey—even if it adds unnecessary weight to their backpack.

Sometimes the extra item will nourish a pilgrim's spirit—like a miniature religious book or a small book of poems. Or a pilgrim with an artist's soul might argue that it's absolutely worth the extra weight to take a sketchpad, special camera gear, or a watercolor painting kit.

If you take something to help sustain your spirit or to otherwise enhance your pilgrimage, be sure to include that item in your backpack when you train for the Camino walk. Then you'll know if it's worth carrying the extra weight.

You could also participate in the Camino's historical traditions (while not adding much weight to your pack) by bringing a stone and a scallop shell from home—or by finding them somewhere along The Way.

Leaving a Stone Behind

Many pilgrims will bring a small stone from home and leave it somewhere along the Camino. Some even paint their name, a word, or a message on that stone.

The reasons for leaving a stone vary from pilgrim to pilgrim. Some might carry the stone to symbolize the carrying of a personal grief. After leaving the stone behind, they hope that helps to leave the grief behind them too. Others will place their stone to mark the spot where the purpose of their journey is fulfilled—after reaching an important decision, or after experiencing an "Aha! That's it!"

moment, for example. And many pilgrims leave their stone on a particular trail marker, like the one that indicates there are only 100 kilometers (about 62 miles) left before arriving in Santiago de Compostela.

On the Camino

One of the most famous sites to leave a stone is called the Cruz de Ferro—an iron cross found on the highest mountain pass on the Camino Francés route. Some have even received a blessing for their stone at a Benedictine monastery in Rabanal del Camino, a village near the Cruz de Ferro (about 230 kilometers away from Santiago de Compostela). If you're interested in the blessing, ask for more information at the pilgrims' refuge next to the monastery, or check your guidebook.

Stones aren't the only mementos pilgrims leave behind at the Cruz de Ferro. You'll also see scribbled notes on torn pieces of paper, photographs, plastic flowers, trinkets, and talismans. It's not surprising to see hiking gear left behind too: the steep climb often prompts the purging of overweight backpacks. And apparently the Cruz de Ferro gets its own purging: I've read that the local municipality occasionally clears the area. With tens of thousands of people walking the Camino Francés each year, that's surely a good idea.

Occasionally you'll see collections of pilgrim mementos at other Camino sites too. I once discovered a remote grotto in Galicia on the Camino Francés route. Inside the dark and damp space I saw hundreds, if not thousands, of personal items left behind. I was inspired to take off my backpack and spend some time looking through the layers of pilgrim artifacts. The piles of notes and trinkets and stones reminded me that I was only one small drop in the river of humanity that has walked *The Way* for a millennium.

For centuries pilgrims have also embraced an enigmatic symbol for the Camino: the scallop shell.

SHELL MOTIF SEEN ON THE TOUR DE VÉSONE—A GALLO-ROMAN TEMPLE IN THE TOWN OF
PERIGUEUX, FRANCE, ON THE VÉZELAY ROUTE

Carrying a Scallop Shell

A scallop shell is the pilgrim's badge—whether you're religious or not. It tells other pilgrims and local citizens you're on your way to Santiago de Compostela—whether you plan to arrive there or not. When you're far from the trail—like at the Madrid airport or on the Paris Metro—and see someone with a scallop shell attached to their backpack, you'll know that backpacker is either on their way to the Camino or on their way home after a Camino pilgrimage.

Pilgrim's Scallop Shell
Spanish = *concha de peregrino*
French = *coquille Saint-Jacques*

171

SCALLOP SHELLS AT A FRENCH PUBLIC MARKET

A Little History

The history for how the shell became a symbol for the Camino has been lost. Nevertheless, there are numerous speculations about its original meaning. One story is this: startled to see the boat carrying the body of the Apostle James (Saint James) approaching the Galician shore, a bridegroom and his horse fell into the sea. By a miracle the saint helped the bridegroom emerge from the sea, and both the bridegroom and the horse were seen covered in scallop shells. Another related version of the story says it was the body of James that was submerged off the coast of Spain, and when it eventually emerged from the sea it was covered in scallop shells. These stories might explain why you'll see numerous sculptures, reliefs, paintings, and stained-glass windows showing Saint James with a scallop shell sewn into his hat or cloak.

But others speculate that the shell was a symbol of the Camino because it was used by pilgrims to gather drinking water, or to hold food provided by local citizens as charity. Yet another idea proposes that the scallop shell's ribs represent the many pilgrimage routes that eventually connect at one point: the destination city of Santiago de Compostela.

Another explanation for why the shell became a Camino symbol suggests that the shell was simply a souvenir, proving that a pilgrim made it all the way to Finisterre (Fisterra in the Galician language) on the Atlantic Ocean in Spain—where scallop shells are naturally found.

Finisterre

Finisterre is the westernmost land point in Europe, and it was considered the end of the earth by early Europeans. It takes about three days to walk there from Santiago de Compostela, and today many pilgrims also finish their pilgrimage at Finisterre. It's tradition to burn your pilgrimage clothing after reaching the shore. A local government council even provides a fire pit for this ritual ending of the old and beginning of something new. Some say the tradition has its roots in the ancient Celtic rituals practiced in that area of Spain.

You might also hear speculations about the scallop shell's meaning long before it became a symbol for the Camino pilgrimage. It was not uncommon for pagan symbols and rituals to be adopted by the early Roman Catholic Church, especially if they already had special meaning for the local inhabitants. So it's possible the symbolic shell image was transformed to its new purpose over a thousand years ago. Some will say the earlier meaning of the shell was connected to the Roman worshippers of Venus. Archaeological digs in an ancient Roman cemetery close to Finisterre have found bronze shells, perhaps supporting that idea in the local context.

But a human connection with the scallop shell goes back even further than the Romans. A Phoenician coin with a scallop-shell motif was recently found in Sagunto, Spain (near the city of Valencia). Even more fascinating is the discovery of scallop shells in two caves near Murcia, Spain (also near Valencia). Archaeologists say those shells were used by Neanderthals about 50,000 years ago to mix pigments—and those archaeologists also say the shells might have been worn as jewelry too. That's about 10,000 years before modern humans arrived on the scene.

So perhaps the only historical certainty about the symbol of the scallop shell is the enduring human affection for it. Maybe the shell's significance was the same for Neanderthals, Phoenicians, Romans, and the early pilgrims to Santiago: they thought the scallop shell was beautiful, so they wore it or used it as a design element.

Scallop Shells Today

Most pilgrims today find some way to display the scallop shell. The most common method is to attach a shell to the backpack. But pilgrims might also wear shell pins, pendants, or necklaces to participate in the Camino tradition of wearing the scallop shell.

Finding a Scallop Shell

Look for a shell to attach to your backpack in tourist shops or Camino association offices at popular Camino departure locations such as Vézelay, Le-Puy-en-Velay, and Saint-Jean-Pied-de-Port in France; and Sevilla, Roncesvalles, Pamplona, or Puente la Reina in Spain.

You might also find a scallop shell at towns or cities located midway on a pilgrimage route, especially at an important and historic pilgrimage site. Look for tourist shops near a cathedral or a large church—they sometimes sell scallop shells. If you're flying into the city of Santiago de Compostela before taking transportation to your pilgrimage starting point, you'll easily find a shell in the medieval part of the city.

You'll also see a variety of pins, pendants, and other jewelry with the shell motif for sale along the most popular Camino routes. Once, when I couldn't find an actual scallop shell, I bought a keychain with a metal shell that was large enough to attach to my backpack. That turned out to be a practical option: there was no chance the metal shell would break like an actual shell might during its precarious life dangling from a Camino backpack.

Finally, there's the gastronomic option: order scallop shells at a restaurant (*vieira* on a Spanish menu, and *coquille Saint-Jacques* on a French menu) and take one with you after your meal. Or go to a fish market and buy one scallop shell. The tricky part is to find a way to drill two holes into the shell so you can attach it to your backpack. Ask around—local citizens are usually happy to help a pilgrim.

Because the scallop shell is the Camino's beloved symbol, you'll see it displayed everywhere—on trail markers, road signs, fenceposts, and in gardens, restaurants, hotels, chapels, churches, and cathedrals. When you see the shell, it often reassures you that you're on the right path. And wearing or carrying the scallop shell indicates that you have joined the historic Camino community of pilgrims who have embarked on a journey to a faraway place, hoping for adventure, fun, spiritual renewal, and, most of all, a safe return home.

AUTHOR'S CAMINO GEAR: BACKPACK WITH SCALLOP SHELL, BASQUE CANE, BLUE FOAM SLEEPING
PAD, AND THAT TEMPORARY 100 PERCENT PAPER HAT

RESOURCES

This list includes all of the websites mentioned throughout the book. I've also added several books about the Camino pilgrimage that might be helpful when planning your own journey.

Also, feel free to contact me if you have specific questions about the Camino or feedback about this book. I'd love to hear from you!

Twitter: @JeanChristie1
Website: www.caminopacklist.com

Pilgrims' Websites

Confraternity of Saint James
www.csj.org.uk

The Confraternity of Saint James is a London-based nonprofit group that is dedicated to helping people organize their own Camino pilgrimage. You can buy guidebooks from their online bookshop for all of the most popular Camino routes—and for many of the less-traveled Camino routes too. You'll also find numerous links on their website, including links to Camino associations throughout the world. Their website is a good place to check for updated information on the Camino in general and for specific routes. I recommend this website as the place to start your search for more information about the Camino.

Camino de Santiago Forums (in English)
www.caminodesantiago.me
www.caminodesantiago.me.uk

These forums provide a platform where you can ask questions or read what others are saying about the Camino. Although they have similar website addresses, these are separate websites, each with their own pilgrims' forum—click "Forum" on the home pages to access them. You'll also find a lot of other helpful information on these websites (including links to other Camino websites).

Caminolinks
www.caminolinks.co.uk

This helpful website provides links to Camino-related websites that are written in English—including links to pilgrims' journals (click "Journal Links") and a few links for artisan walking sticks.

The Pilgrims' Office in the city of Santiago de Compostela
www.peregrinossantiago.es/eng/

This link will take you to the English version of the website that focuses on the Christian spiritual and historical aspects of the Camino. You'll see interactive features showing the details of the Cathedral of Saint James and find Camino statistics showing the approximate (not all pilgrims are counted) number of monthly arrivals at Santiago de Compostela by gender, age, nationality, and other categories. This can be useful information if you're not sure when to walk the Camino: it will show you when is the best time if you want to go alone but want to feel certain that you'll meet others along the way—or if you want to walk at a time that is less busy.

Digital or Print Guidebooks for the Camino (in English)

Confraternity of Saint James
www.csj.org.uk

Publishes Camino route guidebooks for nearly all the routes in a lightweight print format with plastic covers to protect against the rain. Also provides some digital route guides through their website. As of this writing you can find the digital route guides on their site by going to "CSJ Guides and Updates," found under the heading

"Information and Resources" on their home page. You'll find the print guidebooks under the heading "Bookshop."

Cicerone
www.cicerone.co.uk

A great site for walkers and trekkers in general, and a publisher for some of the Camino guidebooks—both in print and in ebook formats. Located in the U.K., but sells internationally.

Camino Apps for Mobile Devices

Be sure to read the fine print: some features of an app may only work with a wireless or cellular connection. This is frequently true for any map-related features. If the maps aren't embedded within the app itself as a part of the download, you'll likely need a connection to use the full functionality of the app—and it's sometimes difficult to get connected in rural parts of the Camino.

Use the keywords "Camino" and "Camino de Santiago" when searching for the latest apps that relate to the Camino de Santiago (a search may not bring up all the options when using just one or the other alone).

Apple iTunes App Store
www.apple.com/itunes/

Go to the iTunes App Store from your computer or mobile device (as of this writing you'll need an Apple device to use the apps).

Android Market
https://market.android.com

You'll need a device that uses the Android operating system.

Amazon's Appstore for Android
www.amazon.com

The Amazon apps are also for devices using the Android operating system.

Suggested Reading

Books About the Camino Experience

These books will help you learn more about what to expect on a Camino pilgrimage.

Gitlitz, David M., and Linda Kay Davidson. *The Pilgrimage Road to Santiago: The Complete Cultural Handbook*. New York: St. Martin's Press, 2000. A classic resource about the most popular pilgrimage route in Spain: the Camino Francés. The book's cover best describes what you'll find inside: "Including art, architecture, geology, history, folklore, saints' lives, flora and fauna."

Mullen, Robert. *Call of the Camino: Myth and Meaning on the Road to Compostela*. Scotland, U.K.: Findhorn Press, 2010. An inspiring account of the author's journey to Santiago de Compostela that also blends well-researched myths, legends, and historical aspects of the Camino with the stories of the pilgrims he's met along the way.

Frey, Nancy Louise. *Pilgrim Stories: On and Off the Road to Santiago*. Berkeley and Los Angeles: University of California Press, 1998. This is an in-depth study of the Camino pilgrim experience by an anthropologist-author. But the book is not a dry, academic read: the author shares stories from many of the hundreds of pilgrims she's met, and not only about their pilgrimage journeys, but also what happens to many of these pilgrims after they return home.

Books Not About the Camino, But Worth Mentioning

Cousineau, Phil. *The Art of Pilgrimage: The Seeker's Guide to Making Travel Sacred*. Berkeley, California: Conari Press, 2000. This book is not specifically about the Camino pilgrimage (although it is mentioned), but it considers the pilgrimage phenomenon as an archetype that has occurred throughout time and place, and for all human beings. This book is one of my favorites, and

I recommend it here since it might inspire you to think about the possibilities for your own pilgrimage—starting with the first chapter, "The Longing" to go…

Jardine, Ray. *Trail Life: Ray Jardine's Lightweight Backpacking.* AdventureLore.com: Adventure Lore Press, 2009. Its focus is on wilderness backpacking, but this book is considered one of the classics according to experienced lightweight backpackers. I've also listed Ray Jardine again below under Making Your Own Backpacking Gear, since this book also has details about how to make some backpacking gear. (Shop around for this book: for some reason I found it listed on major online bookstores with outrageous pricing—from $121 to $900 USD! You can go directly to www.rayjardine.com to get the author's more reasonably priced book.)

Backpack Clothing and Gear

Google the keywords "lightweight backpacking" or "ultralight backpacking" to discover more resources—including your own local shops.

Backpacking Light
www.backpackinglight.com
At this website you'll find backpacking gear reviews and articles, a community forum for lightweight backpackers, and both new and used gear for sale. Some features on the website are by subscription only, but you can also discover a lot of free information and resources. The focus is on wilderness backpacking, but Camino pilgrims might also find helpful information.

REI
www.rei.com
Outdoor gear, in all categories. They have terrific exchange and refund policies, in my experience.

Barrabes
www.barrabes.com

A Spanish website that sells outdoor gear, including the Altus Atmospheric Poncho used by many pilgrims (they have an English-language option for their website). I've not used the poncho myself, but so many pilgrims have recommended this particular poncho that I thought I should mention it.

GoLite
www.golite.com

Specializes in lightweight backpacks, sleeping bags, rain jackets, and other hiking clothes.

Western Mountaineering
www.westernmountaineering.com

Specializes in lightweight down sleeping bags, vests, and jackets.

Rick Steves
www.ricksteves.com

Sells a variety of travel items, including money belts and European maps and guidebooks (though not Camino maps and guidebooks). The website also provides a lot of European travel tips. Email them to find out if they ship directly to your country (they process orders outside the U.S. differently).

J. R. Liggett's
www.jrliggett.com

Multipurpose body soap, shampoo, and laundry soap (don't worry, it's mild!) in an all-in-one bar.

Feet Relief
www.feetrelief.com

Toe gel caps for blisters and other foot-care products. Click on "Products" to navigate your way to the toe gel caps.

Other Suppliers

The following may have limited shipping options outside of North America (or you can try REI, mentioned earlier, which often carries products from these companies):

ExOfficio (www.exofficio.com) for hiking pants, shirts, and underwear, among other travel gear.

Crocs (www.crocs.com) for lightweight alternate footwear.

Making Your Own Backpacking Gear

Ray Jardine
www.rayjardine.com

(Also the author of *Trail Life: Ray Jardine's Lightweight Backpacking*, described earlier under Suggested Reading.)

Ray Jardine's website (and book) offer instructions and kits for making some lightweight backpacking gear—an option that might appeal to those with a limited budget. Jardine's focus is on wilderness backpacking, but his philosophy and techniques can also be applied to Camino backpacking journeys.

Quest Outfitters
www.questoutfitters.com

Outdoor-gear fabrics, patterns, fasteners, zippers, and more for those who want to make their own backpacking gear.

Other Resources

Amazon
www.amazon.com

A good place to find images and reviews of voltage converters and adapters for electronic devices.

Word Reference (translation)
www.wordreference.com

A free online multilingual dictionary, with access to forums where you can ask language-usage questions.

Fabric Link
www.fabriclink.com

This site describes itself as the "Educational Resource for Fabrics, Apparel, Home Furnishings and Care." Click on "Trademark" on the left side of the website's home page to access the Alphabetical Trademark/Brand Name Index. There you can find a long list of human-made fabrics to see what they're made of. That information might be helpful when you're trying to decide between two rain jackets that use different waterproof fabrics—or between two different sleeping bag fills, for example.

VoIP (Voice over Internet Protocol) Calls

These applications can be used to make free or inexpensive international phone calls using computers or mobile devices. This is a competitive technology, so Google "VoIP calls" to search for the best and most up-to-date options.

Skype
www.skype.com

Truphone
www.truphone.com

Viber
www.viber.com

International phones for sale or for rent, or to buy prepaid SIM phone cards before leaving home

Cellular Abroad
www.cellularabroad.com

Planet Omni
www.planetomni.com

Telestial
www.telestial.com

ACKNOWLEDGMENTS

It was my lucky day when by chance I found Amy Scott at Nomad Editorial. Thank you, Amy, for your editing expertise, patience, and attention to the details—and for asking me great questions to clarify the text. I'm grateful for all your help and support throughout this journey.

Thank you to Henry Zoel for the wonderful book cover design, and for being such a delight to work with. I'd also like to thank Susan Zarate at Zarate Graphics for creating the backpack graphic and for fine-tuning some images—and for doing it so quickly! Thanks also to Jeffrey King at Mapping Specialists for designing the Camino map, and to Nancy Cortelyou at Saffron Writes for her proofreading expertise. And to Mary and Mike: that software really helped; thanks!

I'm also grateful to Marcela Calderón-Vodall, Spanish-language librarian at the Seattle Public Library, for finding Spanish and French translations for some technical terms for mobile phones. Thank goodness for public libraries and their expert researchers.

I must also send wishes for a *buen Camino en la vida también* to countless Camino pilgrims met along The Way who were the source for many of the ideas found in this book.

Thank you Charlie, Nancy, and Leah for your comments and suggestions—with extra gratitude to Leah for her patience and flexibility as I worked in the cave. Thank you to Bailey, too, for reading the manuscript so thoroughly! I also appreciate your squeezing that reading into your busy schedule.

And thanks to the memory of Bob Bent, a great pal, sorely missed.

ABOUT THE AUTHOR

Although not particularly athletic, Jean-Christie Ashmore has walked over 2,400 kilometers (about 1,500 miles) on Camino pilgrimage routes in France and Spain. She lives in Seattle with her partner and two sassy cats. Contact Jean-Christie through Twitter @ JeanChristie1 or at www.CaminoPackList.com

68050155R00115

Made in the USA
Lexington, KY
29 September 2017